Running Down a Dream

Running Down a Dream

A MEMOIR

Candy Palmater

HARPERCOLLINS PUBLISHERS LTD

Published by HarperCollins Publishers Ltd

First edition

HarperCollins books may be purchased for educational, business,
or sales promotional use through our Special Markets Department.

HarperCollins Publishers Ltd
Bay Adelaide Centre, East Tower
22 Adelaide Street West, 41st Floor
Toronto, Ontario, Canada
M5H 4E3

www.harpercollins.ca

Library and Archives Canada Cataloguing in Publication information

Title: Running down a dream : a memoir / Candy Palmater.
Names: Palmater, Candy, author.
Description: First edition.
Identifiers: Canadiana (print) 20220278377 | Canadiana (ebook) 20220278407 |
ISBN 9781443455091 (hardcover) | ISBN 9781443455107 (EPUB)
Subjects: LCSH: Palmater, Candy. | LCSH: Entertainers—Canada—Biography. |
LCSH: Comedians—Canada—Biography. | LCSH: Television personalities—Canada—
Biography. | LCSH: Television actors and actresses—Canada—Biography. |
CSH: First Nations women—Canada—Biography. | LCGFT: Autobiographies.
Classification: LCC PN2308.P35 A3 2022 | DDC 792.092—dc23

Printed and bound in the United States of America

LSC/H 9 8 7 6 5 4 3 2 1

For my family, living and dead.
I love you and will be forever in your debt.

I rise
I rise
I rise
—Maya Angelou, "Still I Rise"

Contents

Foreword

The "work" Candy and I did together really wasn't work at all; it was a kind of honour, a healing, a sharing of Candy with the world. She was a very special human who gave more than she received, and gave wholeheartedly, never seeking reciprocation. It seemed her proverbial well of energy and light never drained. It is strange when someone of great significance departs our world yet leaves behind precious treasure. This treasure is the lasting gift of her love, kindness, laughter, intelligence, tenacious spirit and tenderness, and her uncanny ability to hold space for audiences of all sizes and to remember every person she met. Candy was a true medicine woman. Her heart expanded to accommodate people, and she never said no to anyone who needed her. I never fully understood the immensity of Candy, even after twenty-two years as her life and business partner, until now that I am navigating my life without her.

I miss the late-night discussions we would have, often heated, deep and tender. Nighttime was always the safest space to unlock our thoughts and feelings and help one another navigate the complications and confusions of life. To her fans, family and friends, Candy's life appeared easy, and while it was fun, it was far from easy. Candy lived with chronic pain for many years. While hiding the suffering when out in public, she experienced terrible physical agony privately. I was there for her. Her indomitable personality blocked the suffering most times, and she always told me that the energy of other people was healing to her, helping her to forget the intense pain. The excitement of entertaining, speaking or being on set and onstage, was her medicine. Only I knew the truth of her pain, and that no matter how much Candy may have soaked in everyone's energy, she worried there was never enough time to get it all done. And she was right. Candy passed away suddenly at home on December 25, 2021. She had finished writing the manuscript and was working on final edits of this book.

I regret that you won't have the chance to meet her, to see her in her element, to simply be in her presence and fall in love with her beautiful, giving spirit. She was a magnificent force, a beacon of hope. Candy was the love and light in this dark world.

Candy was a strong advocate for so many people. She focused a large amount of her life on helping humans to think outside the box, to love ourselves and one another unconditionally. She travelled as far as New Zealand to provide lessons of personal strength, growth and teamwork. The people at the many schools, colleges, universities, unions and all levels of government where she spoke felt her powerful message of love and kindness through her incredible, candid stories of adversity.

There is so much to say about this unique, special rhinestone of a person, a precious gem that left us way too soon. That early Christmas morning, moments before her death, we had a wonderful exchange of love and gratitude. (We always rose early on Christmas, and I am so glad to have risen that day.) I put on the coffee, as I always did before taking out Pearl, our dog. She was relaxing in bed with book open, all smiles and happiness, peacefully reading, as was her favourite pastime. I left with Pearl for a total of six minutes, and when we returned, I expected to see her in her chair near the Christmas tree. She wasn't there. I called out, no answer. I went to her and she was already gone. Just like that. Like the wind came in and stole her soul.

This memoir is one of her many legacies. Here, Candy shares the personal stories of her earlier years that helped mould her to be the strong, vivacious, sensual woman she fully was. It will help you get to know her deeply and understand how remarkable this human was—a gifted person, and an all-around special human being.

—Denise Tompkins, Candy's widow and manager
April 2022

Preshow Chatter

I am a queer, Indigenous, recovered-lawyer-turned-feminist comic who was raised by bikers in the wilds of northern New Brunswick. I'm fifty-two years old, and it has been one hell of a crazy ride so far.

Since my early thirties, I have been asked numerous times to write a memoir. I always resisted because I felt that I was too young, and I couldn't see how reading my story would be of benefit to anyone. Even if my experiences were extreme, I felt I needed the wisdom of age and perspective to put them in context in a way that would benefit you, dear reader. Now, however, I am fifty-two and I have come to a place in life where I think my story can be helpful. Don't get me wrong: this is no self-help book. You will be scandalized, you will be shocked and you will be entertained, but I think you will also be enlightened. You may find some solace in the bad decisions I've made, and you may find you share more in common with me than you think.

There are three major truths in life that I will explore and revisit all through this book. They are true for me and I believe they are true for you as well.

1. It's never too late.
2. You will fail.
3. You are enough.

A true understanding of these three concepts has enabled me to live an extraordinary life, on my own terms and avoiding boredom and conformity along the way. And maybe, if you embrace these truths, you can, too.

I have, for as long as I can remember, defined success on my own terms as opposed to accepting society's definition. For me, success can be measured by two things: happiness and love. Am I happy most of the time? If not, it's time for a change. For example, I ended my law career to pursue comedy in my early thirties. (Imagine that call home to Mom and Dad.) I did it because practising law was making me *un*happy most of the time. In that same way, I ask myself, Do I feel love? Am I loving myself?

Am I loving those in my life? As I try to get my life to a place where I can answer those questions in the positive, I have always kept the three concepts mentioned above in the forefront of my mind. Let's dive down a bit deeper.

It's never too late. You think it may be too late for you. But honestly, it isn't. In this day and age, there is more emphasis on early accomplishment, so much so that parents are overextending their kids. Preteens have schedules jam-packed with music lessons, sports, acting and so on. I get an eye twitch just thinking about it. If children are expected to peak by age ten, what hope does that leave for a fifty-two-year-old like me . . . a late-blooming fifty-two-year-old at that? I have always been a late bloomer, a slow burn, if you will. I graduated from high school at seventeen years old. I didn't start law school until I was twenty-seven. I performed comedy for the first time at the age of thirty-two in front of a crowd of two hundred women. At forty, I started my television career by launching my own national show called *The Candy Show*. When I was forty-six, my radio career started when I auditioned to be the new host of *q* on CBC radio. And now, at fifty-two, I'm in a TV show and cohosting a morning show, and I have written my first book, which you now have in your hot little hands. What's next? I'm not sure but, trust me, it's never too late.

You will fail. And wow, have I had some spectacular failures in my life. I'm not ashamed of a single one of them. A teacher once told me we use a pencil to do math because it allows us to erase our mistakes. No one expects to get the answer right the first time. At a young age, I figured if this was true for math, it must be true for life as well. Did I fail the bar exam the first time I wrote it? Yes. But John Kennedy Jr. failed it twice before he passed it, and if that rich white boy (may he rest in peace) with all his privilege felt no shame around failing it twice, why should I feel shame around failing it once (during the hardest time in my life, I may add)?

Failure, in my opinion, is the juice of life! It's where all the good stuff is hidden, like easter eggs in a video game. I love it when I win, when things go my way. But I never grow from those experiences. In my life, all my growth has happened during the hard times. It's when I am struggling, when my back is against the wall, that I build character, and it's through those hard times that I have figured out I can do really hard things.

Failure can bring sadness and insecurity. Often, we want to rush through it, sweep it under the rug, forget it as fast as possible. That's a real shame. I think we should linger awhile in our painful places. I embrace the words of Rilke, who encouraged us not to squander our hour of despair. The failures, the pain, the hard times: they are all gifts, things we need to pick up along the way in order to get where we want to go in this life. Even when I am at my lowest, I allow myself to cry for a bit, but then I tell myself this is happening for a reason and I won't be able to figure out what that reason is until I dry my eyes. As you will find out in the pages that follow, I've chosen bad men, the wrong jobs, and in my late teens, I hitchhiked with the wrong truckers! Believe me when I tell you I have had failures. But as I look back on them now, those experiences have all taught me something. I'm not going to lie and say I have no regrets. I really regret acid wash jeans in the eighties. Seriously, though, I think we all have regrets in our lives, things we would do differently if given the chance. But there are no do-overs. The past is gone. If you have kids, they are not your chance to do it over, either. I accept all of my choices, the good and the bad. I know those choices have made me who I am today and they will continue to form and inform me. My job is to learn from those choices and use that knowledge to navigate the failures and mistakes ahead.

To effectively embrace the first two concepts, I've realized that I need to truly believe the third, which is, *You are enough.* It is the hardest of the three truths to accept. Every time I turn on my TV, look at my computer or read a magazine, I'm being told that I am NOT enough. I am not rich enough. I'm not pretty enough. I'm not smart enough. I'm not young enough. I'm not skinny enough. I'm not enough, I'm not enough, I'm not enough.

When I was cheated on, I thought it was because I wasn't pretty enough. When a friend hurt me, I thought it was because I wasn't important enough. Life experience, the advice of Elders and mentors and lots of introspection have allowed me to realize that I am enough. That may sound like an egotistical statement, but it is the very opposite. You must let go of your ego to embrace the concept of being enough. Because, for me, it means accepting my flawed state of being. It means other people's actions toward me are not about me. They are about them. It means—and this is a big one—that what other people think of me is none of my business.

I am still setting goals each day and trying to improve my character, my health and my values, but I do that from a place of knowing that I am enough. It's the only way for me to move forward. When I am in hard times, I hold tight to my three concepts, my questions about happiness and love, and I remind myself that the only way around is through.

This isn't one of those books about a person surviving a horrific childhood and then rising to stratospheric heights. I love those books, but this isn't one of them. I wasn't raised in extreme poverty, although my father was born and raised in a level of poverty most middle-class folks can't even conceptualize, myself included. I was not the victim of crippling abuse as a child, although as a teen, I did deal with the unwanted advances of a man who was old enough to know better, and at twenty years old, I entered a very long relationship with an ex-convict sixteen years my senior. I don't have a deadly disease, but at thirty-eight, I was diagnosed with advanced osteoarthritis, had my first hip replaced at forty and now live with constant pain. I did not grow up to enjoy Oprah Winfrey–size success, but I have been living the life I want to live. And I am enjoying every minute of the ride.

I'm not a shiny, perfect woman who has it all, writing a book about her shiny, perfect life. I'm bruised and dented. I've had some hard knocks and some lucky breaks. I've won some and I've lost some. I've been chasing a dream. That dream is always just around the next corner. I've caught sight of it a few times. I've almost had it in my hands. When I do get hold of a piece of it, I dream a bigger dream. So I will keep chasing, because that dream is out there, ahead of me, and I know it's mine. This book is the story of that dream. In reading it, I hope you are encouraged to step out onto the road and start running down your own dream.

SCENE I

The one where we get the backstory

I can't really tell the story of my own life without first going back and telling the story of my mom and dad. I'm from a little rural area in northern New Brunswick called Point La Nim. Nearby Dalhousie is where my mom and dad grew up and where I attended school.

Dalhousie, New Brunswick, had about six thousand people in it when I was young. It's in the northern part of the province, nestled along the Baie des Chaleur just across from the Gaspé coast of Quebec. The area is inhabited by a mix of Mi'kmaq, francophone and anglophone people, and to outsiders, we all sound a bit French when we speak.

The "front street" is down along the water and is the most important strip in town. The street is actually named William Street, but hardly anyone calls it that. Many of the streets in Dalhousie have colloquial names, like the Convent Hill, the Long Slant and even Gum Rubber Gultch. You know you live in a small town when! Stretching from one end of the front street to the other, blocking the view of the water, was the New Brunswick International Pulp and Paper Mill. It's where the majority of men, and some women, worked when I was a kid. The opposite side of the front street was home to Dalhousie's shopping area. Much of the commerce of the street was domi-nated by a Lebanese family, the Abuds, who came to our town long before I was born. Nazim Abud and his wife owned a large department store that took up a whole block. They ran this store with the help of their adult children. Their son Jimmy (a great musician) ran the furniture and electronics department and George ran the menswear. Daughter Patsy ran womens-wear and Nicole ran the shoe department. Their cousin Phil-lip owned a clothing store a few doors down. My brother Guy worked for the Abuds for many years. But these stores were far too expensive for us. We shopped at The Continental Depart-ment Store and at Dalphens, a discount clothing store. There was an ice cream shop on the front street called the Tastee Freeze. I have such great memories of the Tastee Freeze. Often on a summer evening, my parents would put me in the truck, seated between the two of them, and take me into town for an ice cream cone. I usually had my bath first, so the cab of the truck would be filled with the smell of Halo shampoo and freshly laundered pyjamas. We would get our ice cream and then pull in across the street to watch the traffic and enjoy our treat. My dad would show me how to pound the cone on the palm of my hand to get the ice cream to sink down so that I would have some in every bite right to the bottom of the cone.

Next to the Tastee Freeze was our fried chicken shop called the Dixie Lee. The Dixie Lee is still there and considered almost sacred in my little town. Everyone who has ever moved away misses Dalhousie's Dixie Lee. There are Dixie Lees all over the province of New Brunswick, but none of them compare to Dalhousie's Dixie Lee. Most of us think that is because the late Mrs. Oaks and her daughter Susan made the chicken at our Dixie Lee for forty-seven years and over forty years respectively. These two women are a part of all our lives because they have been frying chicken for us for as long as most of us can remember. There was also a little bar right across from the mill called The Disco 440. I never saw the inside of it because it closed down before I was of age, but my sister Penny worked there as a bartender and my brothers often frequented the place. Also on the front street were a flower shop, a dry cleaner, Lounsbury's car dealership and a very popular restaurant called The Fad.

There is one other part of town that was always bustling back in the day: the Inch Arran, which is the pointy tip of Dalhousie that juts out into the bay. It's named after the Isle of Arran in Scotland, where many immigrants who landed on our shores came from. There is a beautiful lighthouse there. The Lions Club canteen, where we all enjoyed the best french fries in the county, is still there (and we all still love the fries), but the outdoor, in-ground town pool is now gone. The ice hockey rink, which is also home to many of our town gatherings, is located there too, as well as the ball field, where we would go to watch my brother play with the Dalhousie Dodgers. Before my time, there was a beautiful inn located where the rink is now. In the late 1800s, the Intercontinental Railway was constructed and it brought tourism to our town. Inch Arran Inn opened in 1884. Other hotels constructed around that time because of railway tourism include the Algonquin Hotel in St. Andrews, New Brunswick, the Chateau Laurier in Ottawa, Ontario, and the Banff Springs Hotel in Banff, Alberta. Many famous people travelled to the area back then, including Sir John A. and Lady Agnes Macdonald. The inn eventually burned down, but in my time, people like Tom Selleck and Jack Nicklaus travelled to our little corner of the world to fish the Restigouche River.

There is also a camping lot all along the water. In the summer, that lot was always full, not just with people from away, but also town folk who would put their campers up and spend the whole summer by the water.

Dalhousie sits between Eel River Bar First Nation and Point La Nim. Once you pass the Lounsbury's in town, you get on Victoria Street and follow it out of town for a couple of kilometres, and you'll find Point La Nim. It is a settlement of houses situated along the highway between Dalhousie and Campbellton. On the right-hand side, the Baie des Chaleur is very close to the road; on the left is higher country. Just a few minutes out of town, you cross a train track known as Cook's Crossing. Then you will see a sign for Palmater Road. A left-hand turn will take you up a long dirt road that stretches over a steep slope to an opening, at the top of which is where you'll find what I call the Palmater compound: home. It's a cluster of three houses, and behind them, the land reaches back and up again to more mountain terrain.

If you leave Dalhousie in the opposite direction and pass some trees and steep turns, you'll find the small Eel River Bar First Nation nestled along a natural sandbar, with a highway running over it. That stretch of road, like so many of the country roads at home, has its own stories of accidents and early deaths.

My great-grandfather was Louis Thomas Jerome. He was the last hereditary chief in Eel River Bar. At that time, the reserve wasn't located where it is now. It was further down the road in a little place called New Mills. As part of the colonization process, many First Nations in Canada had their land taken and were moved to less valuable bases. Eel River Bar did not escape upheaval. The community was moved from New Mills to the spot where it is located today.

Traditionally, chiefs assumed power through heredity. As I said, my great-grandfather was the last to hold a hereditary chief position in Eel River Bar. Through the Indian Act, the hereditary system was replaced with an electoral system. That system, as legally prescribed to First Nation communities, has created many of the modern-day problems that affect Indigenous peoples. An electoral process is debilitatingly costly and creates an environment ripe for nepotism when it's forced on small communities every two years (which was the case for decades).

My great-grandfather had six children, all girls. Not one of his daughters grew taller than five feet. Obviously, at five foot ten, I got my height from my mother's side of the family. Those daughters were small, but they were pretty tough. My grandmother was one of those six. Her name was Margaret. She married a white man from Toledo, Ohio, named William Palmater. When she married him, according to the law of the time, she lost her status and had to leave the community. Palmater was a logger and a drinker. The New Brunswick International Pulp and Paper Mill had steady work for loggers in the woods surrounding Dalhousie, so he spent a lot of time in the bush, and my grandmother spent a lot of time with other men. She had four sons and a daughter. My dad was the second youngest. The oldest was Frank, then Uncle Lummy (actually, Walter—I didn't find out Lummy was a nickname until I was seventeen!). Then there was a daughter named Dolly, my dad, then his younger brother, John. Although this is mostly family story and not proven, it seems that not all of my grandmother's children were William Palmater's children, although his name appears on all of their birth certificates.

When you look at pictures, all the kids have similarities, but they are also similar to men who were my grandmother's drinking buddies. I always thought my uncle John looked like one of those drinking buddies. That man was also a bit of a father figure to my dad and they remained close friends until the man's death.

My siblings and I look a lot like the children of Eel River Bar Elder Margaret LaBillois. She was known to me my whole life as Aunt Margaret. Her husband and my dad were first cousins, and we were taught to call all relatives older than us Uncle or Aunt. It wasn't until shortly before my father's death that we figured out why we share so many features with the LaBilloises. According to Aunt Margaret, she and Daddy were half-siblings. Apparently, my grandmother had an affair with Margaret's father, Jim Pictou, and my dad was the result. Jim Pictou was originally from Pictou Landing, Nova Scotia, which also explains why there are folks in that community who look a lot like my cousins and me.

Daddy didn't talk about who his father was or about his childhood. It was, by all accounts, very painful. My mother knew some of his secrets, which she insisted she would never share with me. He often said he wished they could develop a pill that would allow him to forget his childhood. This was usually said with tears in his eyes, and then he would shut down.

One story, however, that he told often was about the day the bank locked his family out of their house. He would get a faraway look in his eye, and then he would recount the story as though he was watching a film of it in his mind. Before I share the story with you, here is a little backstory so you understand the context.

When my uncle John was born, William Palmater left. Daddy felt this was because he realized Uncle John was not his child. No one knows for sure why this man, whom I refuse to call my grandfather, chose to abandon his wife and children, but that is exactly what he did. He went back to the United States without a word and apparently started a second family in Ohio. They only heard from him one more time, when Daddy and his brothers were overseas fighting in World War II. He contacted my grandmother and said he wanted to come see them when they returned to Canada. Upon hearing this, my father stayed in Europe for an extra year after the war in order to avoid the meeting—something he regretted for the rest of his life. Eventually, William Palmater died in Ohio. He had never been able to control his drinking, and I understand that he died alone and drunk in the street and lay in the morgue for days before his Ohio family claimed his body.

Left alone with five young children, my grandmother couldn't pay for the house in Dalhousie. The Indian Act prevented her from returning to the reservation.

This is the story that Daddy recalled with complete clarity:

He said it was four o'clock in the afternoon on a cold winter Tuesday when a man from the bank came and evicted them from their house. As Granny and her five children stood desperate on the street, the man from the bank put a lock on the door.

Granny did not weep nor did she beg. She looked at the banker and sternly proclaimed, "You will die with a crooked face." Call it coincidence or call it the curse of a woman done wrong, but that banker had a severe stroke from which he never fully recovered. His face was disfigured by the stroke. He lived the rest of his life, until his death, with a crooked face.

Granny took her kids into the bush and put up a tar paper lean-to. My grandmother was a medicine woman. In modern times, she would be referred to as a midwife or a doula, but back then, women like her were often called baby catchers. Even the doctor in town would bring her with him to home births. It was one of the many ways she scraped together money to keep her kids alive. Along with her midwife earnings, she made high chairs, snowshoes and baskets, which she sold to the white people in town. She had a draw knife that she made herself. It had a blade almost resembling a straight razor. The handle was Lshaped with a small animal face carved into the end of it. With that knife, she could carve a high chair out of a single piece of wood.

My father must have inherited her abilities. I always loved watching my father work with his hands. Whether he was braiding my hair, fixing a motorcycle or putting up a book-shelf, Daddy had elegant hands. They were beautiful to look at. Long, straight fingers. Dark skin smoothly covering visible ten-dons and veins. Smooth, large nail beds with bright half-moons sitting in relief against the dark background. The nails were always clean, buffed and perfectly shaped. And the way he worked with them was elegant as well. Never rough. Almost balletic movements. After my bath, when I would scream as my mom brushed my long, tangled hair (cream rinse and No More Tears wouldn't enter our world until my teens), Daddy would say, "Let me do it." I would sit on the floor between his legs, and he would start pulling those long, elegant fingers through my hair. He never used a brush. He would worry each tangle with his fingers until it magically let go. I can still recall how wonderful it felt when his fingers would then rake all the hair off my face and pull it to the nape of my neck, where he would start the braid. He would always tell me I had such beautiful, thick hair. To this day, whenever I am at the hair salon and someone puts their hands in my hair, that memory envelops me.

One night I was on my way to a high school dance in an outfit I had saved for months to buy. It was a long skirt and long shirt, both in shiny, white brocade. I wore it with a waist-length string of fake pearls and lace tights (give me a break, it was the eighties). As I was getting ready, I caught the skirt and it ripped. There I was with a two-inch tear in this skirt that I hadn't even worn yet. I was as upset as you can imagine a teenage girl being in that situation. Daddy told me to give him the skirt and go finish my makeup. Then he said to Mommy, "Mother, get me a needle and white thread." When I came out of my room perfectly coifed moments later, he had mended the skirt in the floral brocade pattern of the fabric. It was undetectable. Those hands.

Daddy wasn't much of a sleeper, so when I'd come home late at night, he and I would often chat. During one of these talks, at about two in the morning on a warm summer night when I was about nineteen, as I was standing by the foot of his bed, I told him how much I loved watching him work with his hands. He smiled and a bittersweet look took over his face as he said, "I wish you could've seen my mother work with her hands. She could make anything with a piece of wood and her draw knife. I used to love watching her work."

As I'm writing this, I'm looking at that very draw knife on the wall in front of me. It's in a picture box, above the only photo of my grandmother, who died long before I was born. This woman who, as a single Indigenous mother in the 1920s, managed to keep her kids alive. In the picture, she is tiny, but she sure does look tough. Although I never met her, I suspect I got some of my tenacity form her.

My mother told me that Granny Palmater taught her so much about cooking and caring for her children. My older brothers and sisters insist I missed out on our best family treat. Granny would be on the beach with all the kids, and she would mix up a cake batter in a big wooden bowl. Not measuring, of course, just knowing how things should feel and look. She would then pour the batter right onto the hot sand and coals. The kids would get so impatient as she threw hot sand and coals on top of the batter. Then, when the time was right, and of course she knew exactly when the time was right, she would reach down with her bare fingers and grab the cake out of the sand and coals. She held it with one hand and hit it with the other. As she hit it, all the coals and sand would fall away and she was left with a perfect, golden cake that she would then tear up and distribute to my siblings.

Granny kept her children together, and not just her own. In the traditional Indigenous way, she informally adopted my aunt Dixie and raised her as her own. In Indigenous communities, children were seldom formally adopted. If a mom wasn't up to the job, someone would raise the child, but the child always knew who their biological mom was. Mommy gave Granny credit for teaching her how to cook and care for her babies, but she also said that she was not affectionate. She was not a soft woman. Granny was a heavy drinker. I can't say I'm surprised by those facts given the world she had to navigate and survive at the time.

This was the life my father was born into. He was raised without a father and with limited affection. Whatever transpired in that time left a lasting impression on him and shaped the way he would think about women for the rest of his life. Instead of crediting his mother for staying and keeping them alive, he blamed her for his being raised without a father. He felt that if she had been a "good woman" who didn't drink or sleep with other men, his life would have been different. He couldn't see that William Palmater, having abandoned them, was the bad guy in this scenario.

It was so hard to get Daddy to talk about his youth. He didn't begin telling me this next story until he was in his seventies, but then he told it again and again, and it has always haunted me. I've never been able to figure out if it was a dream or if it really happened to him. Maybe when a memory is incredibly painful, it sticks. This story took place shortly after his father left them. He was about three, and his brother John under one, and they were out in a boat. We are surrounded by water in northern New Brunswick, so we all spend lots of time in canoes and boats. I'm not sure who was in the boat with him, but he said he saw a man walking along the shore. And he was convinced that it was his dad. He was so excited that when the boat got close enough to shore, he jumped out and swam in and went running up to the man. But when he got close to him, he realized it wasn't his father at all. Every time he told me that story, he became incredibly emotional, so I know that being raised without a father had a profound impact on him.

He had his grandfather for a short time and he was very close to him. When he was eight or nine, he would walk from town, over the mountain and through the woods to get to the reserve, about a three-kilometre walk over rough terrain. I can't even imagine a nine-year-old making that walk, not to mention making it alone. My great-grandfather had a small shack located where my Aunt Margaret's house is now. When Daddy arrived at the shack hungry (my father spent the majority of his childhood hungry), his grandfather always had a piece of dried fish or dried ham. Great-grandfather would take out his jackknife and cut Daddy a piece of the meat, which he would hand to him with what Daddy referred to as "biscuit," but was likely a piece of luskinigan (traditional Mi'kmaq bread made with just flour, salt and water). Daddy talked about that meagre meal as though it were a feast shared by two kings. It was a rare positive memory of his young life. Unfortunately, my great-grandfather died when Daddy was only twelve, and so he was left, then, as a young boy, to figure out how to be a man on his own. All things considered, he did a great job, but that childhood would affect the rest of his life, and the damage it caused to him had ripple effects that touch my entire family to this day.

As my father was growing up with those experiences, my mother, who was white, was growing up with her mom and dad in Dalhousie. Her father was a quiet and submissive man, built long and lean. Mommy, also quiet and submissive, was very close to him. Her mother (the only grandparent still alive when I was born) was a very big woman with a personality to match. She was definitely the dominant person in their marriage. My grandmother died when I was four. They tried to perform an autopsy, but they told my mother all her organs were encased in fat, and on her death certificate, they indicated that she died of complications related to obesity.

My memories of Granny Foster are limited because I was so young when she died. I do remember how big she was, and how warm and wonderful that felt when I put my arms around her. When we would go to her house for a visit, she'd bring me into the kitchen, get out a slice of white, store-bought bread, slather it with butter and Kraft raspberry jam, and then she would cut it into four little squares, put it on a plate and set it on the table next to a glass of milk. I would climb up onto the chair, full of anticipation, knowing how delicious it was going to taste. Granny had large breasts, which she liked to rest on the table in front of her. She put pin curls in her hair, as did my mom, and she laughed easy. However, while she may have laughed and joked, she didn't play. Make no mistake, she was the boss. When I was young, I was confident and already asking some of the harder questions in life. I used to ask my mom why she and I were so different, and she would say, "If my mom had lived long enough for you to really know her, you would see where your personality comes from."

Granny and Grampy Foster had four children. First came Aunt Dora, followed by my mom, then Uncle Pat and Uncle Donald. Aunt Dora was dominant, like her mom. When I was young, I loved it when she would visit. She laughed a lot and she reminded me of my sister Sharron. Uncle Pat was my favourite uncle. He was a gentle giant. Huge and kind with twinkling, blue eyes. The youngest was Uncle Donald—the only living sibling of either of my parents. Uncle Donald was also sweet, and we were close to him and Aunt Carol, until they divorced and then we didn't see Uncle Donald or my cousin Wendy as much anymore.

Nicknames were obviously a big thing in that little town because, just like Uncle Lummy, Uncle Pat also had a different name on his birth certificate. It wasn't until I was in my early forties that I realized my uncle Pat's real name was Earl.

My mom's family wasn't rich, but they always had food and a roof over their heads. She never experienced hunger the way my dad did. It wasn't until my mom's teen years that things got hard.

That's when my grandfather got tuberculosis and went into a sanatorium. My grandmother opened a little store in the sun porch of their house on Goderich Street in order to earn money. Every year of my life, we have tied our Christmas turkey with the same ball of twine she used to use in her store.

Even with the store, there wasn't enough money, so my mom and her sister, Dora, ended their educations and went to work as housekeepers in other people's homes. Our town had a large port where ships would come from all over the world to pick up loads from the pulp and paper mill. Uncle Pat, who was only fourteen at the time, took work on one of those ships. He sailed away and started his adult life and never returned. He settled in Timiskaming, Ontario, where my mom and I would visit him and his family until his death ten years ago. I remember how kind he was, how he would cook me mountains of bacon for breakfast and how beautiful I thought his kids were. I can remember making flowers out of coloured Kleenex (very popular in the seventies) for my cousin Barb's wedding. She was the only blonde I remember in our family when I was young, and I thought she was so glamourous.

My mother was close to her father. He was quiet, like her. She was proud of him. He was the kind of man who made good choices, and in this era, we would refer to him as a safe man.

That was important to Mommy because she had such a strong sense of values. It was a loving home with no violence, but I suspect my mom was a bit invisible in that house. Her sister, Dora, was a more dominant personality, as was her mother. After her father died, I think she lost her ally.

I know she loved her mother, but when Granny died and I was so scared of the idea that moms could die, Mommy told me that when that time came, it would not seem as traumatic to me because I would be a grown woman with a family of my own. Mommy died when I was forty-nine years old and it gutted me. I am still not over it, so I have to assume that her feelings for her mother were not as intense as mine were (and are) for her.

Mom was always family oriented. After her parents died, she kept in contact with her siblings, arranging visits to each of them. I know all my cousins. Her siblings did not keep in close contact with one another, however. Some of my first cousins have never met. For me, visiting cousins in the summer was my favourite thing! Mommy and I would ride the train to Montreal every summer to visit Aunt Dodo and Uncle Ringo (actually, my much older cousins, so "aunt" and "uncle," and once again, nicknames, for Doris and Raymond). Dodo was Uncle John's daughter, tiny and tough as nails. She had five kids and worked as a waitress at a popular Montreal restaurant. She made the best spaghetti sauce. At first they lived in LaSalle and later moved to Chateauguay, where they had a pool in the backyard—heaven for this small-town girl.

For me, love of family didn't stop at my immediate family. My cousins were such a rich part of my childhood, and I loved being part of such a large clan. Uncle Pat and Aunt Ginette have passed on, but there are still a bunch of cousins up in Timiskaming, and after the Covid craziness, I hope to make a trip up to reconnect with them.

Mommy and Daddy met when she was six and he was nine. They played baseball together. I would find out later that my athletic ability came from my mother. She was one hell of a baseball player and she could run like the wind.

Mommy witnessed a lot of Daddy's childhood. While I think my mom knew more than any of us, I suspect she didn't know the full extent of the horrors of my dad's experiences. My older brothers and sisters probably know more than I do, and they will likely never share it all with me.

Neither of my parents had an easy life. When World War II broke out, they both got involved in the war effort. My mom stayed in Canada, where she made bullets in a factory, and Daddy, who had lied about his age, went overseas at seventeen to fight. After the war, they ended up back on the North Shore together. They went on a date to the movies. Daddy tried to kiss her good night. She said no. Daddy asked her to marry him that very same night! She said yes. Good grief! I'm a "take it for a test drive" kind of girl myself; obviously not Mommy! She'd had a crush on Daddy from the time she was very young. She didn't have very much experience with men, but she knew she wanted children. She always told me it wasn't actually a husband she wanted so badly; she couldn't wait to get married so she could have children. From the time I was young, she made sure I knew that a "smart girl like me in these modern times" did not need a husband to be a mother. She reassured me that it was something I could do on my own. This is one of the many gifts she bestowed on me that resulted in my fierce independence and the confidence to live my life on my own terms.

Granny and Grampy Foster did not share my mom's enthusiasm for the marriage. The idea of their white daughter marrying a Mi'kmaw man was more than they could handle. It was ironic that her parents did not approve of the match, because my mother's father had been raised by the only Black man in the town of Dalhousie in the 1890s. His name was Fred Johnson. He worked on the railroads, and my great-grandmother married him after her first husband died. Interestingly, my mom's sister, Dora, married a Lebanese man, so the women on my mom's side of the family were ahead of their time when it came to race relations!

My mom and dad eloped to Montreal. The "wedding party" included Daddy's mom and a couple of his drinking buddies. My father was an alcoholic. He had his first drink with his own mother when he was ten, and by the time of my parents' marriage, he was a full-blown alcoholic. Daddy bought my mom a wedding ring in a pawn shop in Montreal for twenty bucks. She wore that ring through hell and high water for sixty-five years until she couldn't slide it over her arthritic knuckles anymore. Now I wear it around my neck on a chain. I had it made into a piece of jewellery that has a pearl in it, because my mother's name was Pearl.

Mommy wasn't wise to the ways of men when she married. She hadn't even had an opened-mouth kiss at the time of her wedding. She found herself miles away from her estranged parents; it was her wedding night and her husband was an alcoholic and, she would later discover, a womanizer. The wedding night was a nightmare for her, something he didn't seem to realize until his seventies. I used to discuss it with both of them in my adult life (their marriage fascinated me). All that aside, they were both happy in their own way. She loved him and couldn't wait to have children. He loved her and always thought she was out of his league, but now she was his wife. It may not be the stuff of romance novels, but it was the beginning of a marriage that lasted over sixty years, until the day Daddy died.

They lived in a shack in Dalhousie that I guess you could call a "two-room," but in reality, the only thing dividing the rooms was a sheet of tar paper. It was located in an area that I mentioned is commonly known as Gum Rubber Gultch. My brother Billy was her first-born. He was born in hospital, but my father was on a "bender" and wasn't there. The next day, he arrived at the hospital, still drunk, with a woman on his arm, to see his first-born son. That would have been it for me, but my mother hung in there. Although years later, when my brother

Billy died and my father was going on about his son, she would give him side eye and say, "'*His son.*' He wasn't even there when Billy was born."

A year later, my brother Sidney was born. He was born at home because, once again, Daddy was out on a drunk and she couldn't get to the hospital. I was half an ounce short of eleven pounds at birth, but she swears Sidney was bigger. We will never know because he never was weighed. In fact, Sidney was in his late fifties before he ever spent a night in the hospital. And to this day, at the age of seventy-two, he has never been on an airplane.

Two years later, Mommy was seven months pregnant with my sister Penny. She was washing clothes in an old tin washing tub with a washboard. In her housedress, she stepped out into a New Brunswick winter snowstorm to empty the tub. In doing so, she fell down an embankment and broke her leg. She lay there in her housedress in the snow, very pregnant and screaming until someone found her and got her to the hospital. At the hospital, she told the doctors they would have to get a cast on her quickly as she had to get home to take care of her two babies. Once again, Daddy was out drinking so it was up to her and her alone to take care of things at home. When I asked her how she managed with a full leg cast while pregnant and with two small children at home, she acted like it was no big thing. She said, "Well, they put me in a full-leg cast, and I just threw that leg over the back of a chair and dragged it around with me so I could do my housework." I mean, it was a different time back then, but it's always fascinated me what she had to put up with in the marriage. The life they had together when he was drinking was difficult and tumultuous. But she stayed and she lived for her children. I often told her I wished I could rewrite her life. Each time she said, "Oh no, I would never change any of it, because if I changed anything, I wouldn't have had you children."

After my sister Penny was born, there was a welcomed reprieve from pregnancy for a few years. Then along came my brother Baby Guy. There we go with nicknames again. His name was Guy, but that was also my dad's name, so my brother quickly became Baby Guy. My father was about five feet, eight inches tall and weighed about 170 pounds. Baby Guy is six feet, three inches tall and about 300 pounds, which makes the nickname rather ironic.

After Baby Guy, my brother Bruce was born. Often when I talk about being the youngest of seven, people are confused about who the seventh is, because Bruce died in infancy. But I always include him because he was my brother. He had Down Syndrome, although they termed it "severe mongolism" at the time. He had red hair, and he had one too many fingers and one too few toes. His hands had grown together into little fists—he couldn't open them up. He cried the whole time he was alive. They told my mother to just leave him at the hospital and go home and try to get pregnant again. She was appalled by this thought. She brought him home and loved him until he died three months later. He is not buried with the rest of my family because he was not baptised. He's in an unmarked grave beneath a walkway outside the graveyard. I'm not sure exactly where he is along the walkway, but there he lies, underfoot and unmarked.

Bruce only lived for three months, but his existence had a profound impact on my family. My father convinced himself that his son's illness was a result of his own drinking. No doctors could convince him otherwise. It took him a few years to get there, but by the time my sister Sharron was born, my father had stopped drinking. When Daddy died, he was fifty-one years sober, which is something I've always been so proud of.

By the time I came along, my mom was forty-three and my dad was forty-six. Because I was born twenty-one years after the first baby and eleven years after the one before me, everyone assumed I was a mistake. My mother often told me, however, that I was actually the only planned baby. The reason for planning my grand entrance was that my father had recovered from alcoholism and ten years had passed, during which they were able to find some financial stability. They both had their own motivation for wanting one more child in that environment.

Mommy loved the idea of having a child she could take her time with and spoil. When the first six came, she often said, she was so busy just trying to keep them all fed and alive and didn't have the resources to spoil them. For Daddy, the motivation was a bit different. He was sober and he had bought a homestead. He wanted a redemption baby. Well, as someone once said, "Be careful what you wish for." He asked the universe for a baby in his later life. And the universe obliged. He got a baby with his personality exactly . . . except that baby was a girl. This was something he would never fully make peace with . . . and neither would I.

My dad had some funny ideas about women. He was an old-school male chauvinist. He wore the pants in our family without a doubt, and he had some very twisted ideas about what "a lady" did and did not do. My father made it clear to me that ladies didn't chew gum in public, they didn't smoke on the street, they didn't swear, they didn't wear dark makeup or short shorts, and although he didn't express it explicitly, he made it clear that ladies didn't have orgasms either! I'd figured out by my teens that being a lady was no fun at all. And besides, I had already figured out how to have orgasms on my own, but it's not time for that story yet.

His childhood played a big part in his twisted thinking, as I mentioned. He was raised by this woman who had a strong sexual identity. The man he thought was his father had left, and because he may have seen that departure as his mother's fault, he developed a classic Madonna-whore concept of women. You marry a Madonna. You do the "dirty" stuff with the whore, or the gumar as they put it in *The Sopranos*. His own mother reinforced this thinking. She told him to "run around with whoever you want to run around with, but when it's time for you to get married, you have to pick a clean, wholesome woman to have your children with."

And that's how he saw my mother. The ideal wife. She was white—my father suffered from internalized racism to a fairly severe degree—she didn't drink, she was wholesome, and she had no sexual experience. She was quiet and subservient. She kept a clean house and took good care of his children. As per his definition of a good wife, she never denied him sex but didn't have fun while "doing her duty." As a result, in many ways, he thought she was too good for him. He put her on a pedestal. But this also meant he kept her separate from a part of his life that he never wanted to sully her with. For most of their married life, he kept a gumar.

This was so complicated, and I think it really confused my view of men and relationships. When I was really young, I loved Daddy in that special way little girls love their daddies. I thought he was infallible. He was chauvinist but he thought I should be Prime Minister. I was eighteen when I found out he had cheated on my mother . . . often. It felt like he had cheated on me. My mom tried to convince me that their marriage was not my business and that I should only judge him on what kind of father he was. But I couldn't get past that feeling of being cheated on. Until that moment, I had believed that my older brother Billy and I were his favourites. I was so confident knowing I was special to him. He picked me. After finding out about his cheating, I never trusted a man again. It had a profound impact on all my relationships with men and had a lot to do with why I thought I would never get married. In the end, I got married, but to a woman.

I know my father loved my mother very, very much. He told me often that his sobriety might not have been possible without her sticking by him all those years.

But at the same time, my father was a ladies' man. And he was pretty easy on the eyes in his younger years. He was old my whole life, so I once asked Mommy why she married him. He was bald and he had no butt. "Why," I asked her, "would you be attracted to that?" She said, "Wait right there," and she ran into the bedroom and she got this picture, and it was him sitting on this motorcycle with his sleeves rolled up and this beautiful head of thick, black hair. And this gorgeous face with these deep dimples, and the vascular, muscular arms. And you could see how thick his chest was and how thin his waist was and the tattoos on his arms. Silver rings on his long fingers. It was interesting, because in that very moment, I looked at the picture and I looked at Mom, and I realized, "Oh my God, he was a bad boy." It had never dawned on me that my mother and I had the same taste in men. My mother and I are two very different people. I have more of my father's personality, but she and I shared the same taste in men, which is why I think that when I spent so many of my early years with my own "bad boy," my mother was always understanding. Even though my whole family railed against me, she didn't. Because she married her bad boy and stood by him, through thick and thin and through ups and downs.

So that was the world that I was born into. When it came time to do my mom's eulogy, I started by saying, "The thing is, she was a saint." It might sound to someone who didn't know her like I was gilding the lily, but I wasn't. So strong were her values that she stood by my father through the worst years of his life because at the tender age of nineteen, she made a commitment to him. My mother was a rock. Steady, strong and unbreakable. She was just such a good mother. Each one of us, her children, felt like we were her favourite. She never tried to live her life vicariously through her children. We never wondered if she loved us. My dad loved me, but there was a lot of pressure and responsibility that came with that love, and when I took a wrong step, a faulty step, he could withhold that love. I started my life squarely in the centre of my father's spotlight. And my father's spotlight was a glorious, warm and wonderful place to be. But it only would take one mistake, like being caught downtown with mascara on, before he would turn that light out and it would get very, very cold. His love and light needed to be earned. All my brothers and sisters would agree, however, that my mother loved us when we were up and she loved us when we were down. She didn't try to tell us how to live our lives. She tried to teach us about values and she suggested we should live by those values, but ultimately, we all knew that we were loved by her regardless.

It's hard to pick one memory of my mother's love—there were so many. I could, in fact, write an entire book of just memories of her. But if I were to pick one memory of my childhood that represents how loved she made me feel, it would be the story of the raspberries. This is not a one-time memory; this is something that happened again and again. In the summer, my mom made me a bedtime snack of raspberries and canned milk. As a young adult, I used to try to replicate it. I would go to the grocery store in the summer and buy some raspberries, some canned milk and a loaf of their store-baked bread. I would go back to my apartment, and I would mix the raspberries and canned milk with some sugar, just like she used to. But every time I ate it, it would not taste like it did when she made it for me as a child. I finally realized it was because what I was remembering was not a taste—it was the entire ceremony of the day.

We lived on a mountain, which I will explain in the next chapter. There were no other kids around. It was just me and Mommy all summer long. In the morning, we'd get up on this beautiful land. She would put a load in the washing machine, which included my Raggedy Ann and Andy bedsheets, and then before the sun even got a quarter of the way up the sky, she'd have those sheets out on the line. Then she would start working in her raspberry patch in the backyard. My mom was tall, with long legs, and I'd see her bent over at the waist for hours picking raspberries and weeding the patch with the early-morning sun beating down on her.

My mother's skin, when the sun beat on it, had the most beautiful smell. She smelled like earth and love to me. I used to love just burying my face in her tanned, warm arms and inhaling that smell until I thought my lungs might burst. The day would be spent out in the sun, and by late afternoon, the east wind would come around as it always did and get those sheets snapping.

At 5:00 p.m. sharp, she would put supper on the table for Daddy and me. And a few hours after supper, once she had the dishes all cleaned up, she'd bring the clothes in, fold them up, put those beautiful fresh sheets on my bed and then draw my bath. Although we didn't have a lot of money, she would always put a little extra Mr. Bubble in my bath. After the bath, she combed my long hair into these beautiful ringlets. She would pull my fresh pyjamas over my head, and I would breathe in the smell of the east wind passing over my little nose.

Then I would run to the table and wait for the best part. Out would come a short little glass with hearts, clubs, spades and diamonds all over it. She used to get mustard in them. There were short ones and tall ones, and we'd use them as drinking glasses. In the short glass, she would put some of those fresh raspberries she had just pulled off the bushes that afternoon. And she'd pour some canned milk over them and put a little bit of sugar in and mush them up with a fork. And then she would cut a slice of homemade bread that she had made in the heat of summer in our kitchen. And as I was sitting at the table in my freshly dried pyjamas and my hair in long, wet ringlets, she would present me with my treat and then sit with me while I ate it. It was then time to brush my teeth and say my prayers, after which she would tuck me in and sit on the edge of my bed, singing "Billy Boy" until I drifted off to sleep.

That was what it was like having Pearl Palmater as a mother. It took me a long time to realize that I can buy all the raspberries and canned milk in the world, and I will never be able to replicate what I now realize was the taste of my mother's love.

Love is what I remember most about my childhood, even with the bikers and hunters, the family fights and family make-ups, and the deaths. It wasn't always easy but it was beautiful. Like life, if it was a beautiful struggle.

SCENE 2

The one where my father is hit by a freight train

When my father got sober, he knew he needed to separate himself from the people with whom he was drinking. In Point La Nim, there was an old man named Mr. Grimmer who owned a farm in an area that was colloquially known as Cook's Crossing. My father bought the farm from Mr. Grimmer. The farm was at the top of a hill and stretched over 135 acres, including some of the Appalachian Mountains. As a kid I always wished I was from town. Now, as an adult, I cherish the compound up on the mountain. And I proudly say I'm "hill people." Every morning when I'm home, I walk out into the sun porch with my morning coffee and look out over the water and the mountains of the Gaspé coast of Quebec, and I ask the same question: "Was this here when I was growing up?" Of course it was, but with the impatience of the young, I couldn't wait to get away from that little town. Now that I live in Toronto, I can't wait to get home to the compound for visits.

In order to get to the farm, you have to leave the highway and drive up a dirt road that winds up a hill. The road is still a dirt road, but it is now officially on the map as Palmater Road. When I was a child, it was considered a private road, so my dad had to clear the snow himself. Halfway up that road was a train track. The track started down by the water in Dalhousie, wound out of town and crossed the main road at Cook's Crossing. From there, it climbed steadily to where it intersected with our road. Long before my time, as I mentioned earlier, that track brought many dignitaries to our little town. Everyone from royalty to prime ministers stayed at the Inch Arran Inn. When train travel ceased to be glamorous or novel, that track became more of an industrial transport system. The train track ran from places like the paper mill, the thermal plant and the CIL chemical treatment plant to destinations across Canada. The trains ran constantly, day and night, pulling freight from those different plants through our property.

During the day, it was usually pulp and paper products. When we heard the whistles blowing at night, we always assumed they were carrying the more dangerous chemicals from the CIL and the thermal plant. Technically, the track was owned then by CN Rail. But it ran right through our property and crossed our road. CN would not put lights or a sign saying there was a track there, because it crossed what was considered a private road. Also, the government would not plow the road.

When I was a kid, northern New Brunswick winters meant I started to ski in early November and I skied until late April. We had snow, and lots of it! The snowbanks in our front yard were so high that in pictures of me standing on them when I was about four years old, the little peak of my hood is nearly touching the electrical wires.

Because there was so much snow, Daddy was always on his tractor, plowing. He had an old tractor, a tractor that had tank treads, sometimes known as caterpillar tracks, instead of tires. There's no way to move quickly when you're on those. And rather than a steering wheel, the tractor had two long sticks that came up—big metal poles—and you moved those back and forth to go forward or backward and to operate the snow scoop on the front. The tractor was yellow. It had an open cab, where my father sat. There was a little yellow roof above him set on four posts, one on each corner, but he was exposed to the weather and elements. Every single time it snowed, Daddy had to plow the road for us or we would have no hope of getting our cars up the hill.

We were always wary of the train. If we knew we had company coming, we would remind them of the track to ensure they checked for trains before proceeding over it. And we always worried when Daddy was on the tractor. In fact, as soon as the train whistle blew, my mother would say, "Where's your father?" Whoever was around would look out the window to see if we could catch sight of Daddy. Most of the time, the reply would be, "Oh, he's in the side yard," "Oh, we see him in the front yard" or "Oh, he's going into the shop."

My mother and I were attached at the hip for the first five years of my life. It was never a surprise to her that I eventually became a professional speaker, because as a child, I never stopped talking. The woman had no peace. My dad used to wonder out loud how my mother put up with it, because from the moment my eyes opened in the morning until they closed before bed, I was talking. Part of Mommy's coping mechanism was to tune me out. If she was knitting or reading one of her Harlequin romances, I would talk to her, and she would nod and respond, but I could tell when she wasn't actually listening to me. I would say crazy, outlandish things like "I'm pregnant" or "I'm going to the moon," just to see if she was listening, because quite often, she'd say, "That's nice, dear." At that point, she was caught and I would call her out for not being focused on me. Good Lord, that is a whole other story. Imagine what that poor woman had to go through with me demanding her attention 24-7. It kind of embarrasses me when I think about it now, but such was the nature of who I was as a kid.

So, on this particular day, it was super snowy, and I think I might have been home from school for a snow day, because I was five, and I was definitely in school by then. Mommy was sitting in the corner chair and she was reading a Harlequin romance. We had a big picture window in the living room that looked out onto the Baie des Chaleur and gave us a clear view down the road to that train track. We could see the train when it went by. The whistle blew, and my mother said, without even looking up from her book, because it was just so automatic, "Where's your father?" As Mommy and I were the only two people in the house, when she said "Where's your father?" I got up on my knees on the couch and looked out the window. Through the heavily falling snow, I could see my dad's tractor. And I could see that my dad's tractor was on the tracks. As I looked, I just had time to register seeing the tractor—and then, where the tractor had been, there was the train. And when the train hit the tractor, the tractor looked like a cardboard box being pushed for a few seconds and then flying through the air. In response to my mother's query, "Where's your father?" I said, "He's just been hit by the train." My mother slammed her book shut and said, "Candy, never say something like that! I understand when you say funny things, but it's not funny to say something like that just to get my attention." With eyes as big as saucers and without tears, I turned my head toward Mommy. In an eerily calm, five-year-old voice, I said, "I'm not making it up. Daddy just got hit by the train."

Mommy stood up but I still think part of her was convinced I was making it up. As she stood, my head swivelled back toward the horror I had just seen. Her gaze followed mine as she turned toward the window and realized the train was coming to a stop.

All of that seemed like a movie playing on slow speed, and then suddenly the video was put in fast-forward! She screamed at me to wait in the house. I was frozen in place, on my knees, on the couch, as I heard her footsteps thundering down the basement stairs toward the door that led out front. There was no sound for a few seconds while she was shoving her feet into boots and grabbing a coat. Then I heard the basement door slam. In the dead quiet of the house, I saw my mother, through the peaceful snowflakes, running down the hill and then disappearing out of sight along the tracks.

I can only imagine what was running through her mind at that moment. She would have been thinking about what her five-year-old, who was all alone in the house, had just witnessed. She would have been sure she was about to see her fifty-one-year-old husband dead, because, I mean, who gets hit by a freight train and lives? She would be wondering what she was going to do as a forty-eight-year-old single mother of a five-year-old, living on a mountain with no driver's licence and no job. But in the next moment, she would be reminded of just how tough her man was. She saw him standing in the snow next to his mangled tractor, blood leaking out of him and staining the pristine snow.

I don't remember them coming up the hill. I remember sitting halfway down the basement steps, scared to go any closer to Daddy because he looked like a movie monster to me. He was covered in snow and blood, and his snow pants were torn open in a mess of blood and material. And Daddy was mad, really mad. He was talking about what it was going to cost him. When you get hit by the train, you're technically on their property, and you slow down their delivery; therefore, you pay a fine. And sure enough, after the accident, CN presented him with a bill!

Later, when we talked about it, he said he had looked both ways twice and then he proceeded. When facing downhill, the view on the right was tricky. The track snaked around the contours of the mountain and visibility was less than twenty feet. As he proceeded forward, he turned his head for one more peek to the right, and the train was there. He said it was so close that he couldn't even see the entire face of the train; he could only see from the light down. With those caterpillar tracks under him, there was no putting the pedal to the metal—he knew he was going to be hit and there was nothing he could do about it. He braced himself as the train overtook him. It crumpled the tractor as though it were a cardboard box, just like I saw from the window. The tractor was caught on the front of the train and dragged along the track, and then, miraculously, he was thrown clear. When he was thrown, one of those big metal poles that are used to steer the tractor went in right at his groin and ripped him wide open from his groin to his knee. The engineer in the train hadn't even seen him; the only reason they stopped was because hitting him busted a fuel line. That's what stopped the train.

He walked up the hill on his own steam, after all that, and was stomping around in the basement getting paler and paler as the blood drained out of him. Finally, my mother said, "Guy, we have to call an ambulance. You're whiter than I am."

His final word before leaving the property was to bark at my brother Sidney, who had come over to help: "Get that tractor out of the ditch and up this hill!" With the train still stopped on the track and the storm still blazing, my brother Sidney got to the task of recovering my father's tractor from the tracks. He had to haul down a huge jack and jack it up off the tracks. Meanwhile, the ambulance couldn't come up to get Daddy because the train was blocking the road. So, still bleeding, Daddy had to walk back down the hill and climb through the stalled train cars to get to the waiting ambulance.

When Daddy was brought to the hospital, he was non-responsive, but he swears he could hear them talking. They were saying, "We're losing him! We're losing him!" He said that in his mind, he was screaming, "NO! I'm still here. Keep working!" Then everything went blank. He flatlined and was brought back to the land of the living via defibrillator paddles.

Now that Daddy's gone, what I really regret is never asking him later in life how this impacted him emotionally. Like all the other traumas my father had suffered in his life . . . emotional traumas, physical traumas, World War II . . . it was just never discussed again. I don't know if he had nightmares. I mean, how many people get hit by a freight train and live? He must have had nightmares. He must have had some kind of PTSD from that. But of course, at that time, we didn't know what PTSD was. My dad just took life's blows and kept on fighting. It was the only way he knew. He never did speak about it. He had the most gruesome scar. It was a valley in his leg that never filled back in. That muscle was cut right to the thigh bone. And I remember, when he had both his knees replaced, getting a glimpse at the bottom part of that scar and how angry-looking it was. But even then, I never actually said to him, "Daddy, does that haunt you? Do you think about it?" So, now, at fifty-two, what haunts me more than actually having been a witness is the fact that I never, even once I became an adult, thought to ask him how he was doing around that. It was just something that happened, and he got through it, and he carried on. But, you know, all those times I found my father sitting in his truck on the beach, just looking at the ocean, I wonder if that wasn't one of the things he thought about. He spent so much time in his head, but he just never shared it with us.

After the accident, life went back to normal on the mountain. When Daddy first bought the land, he moved the family into the old farmhouse that was there. When I was three, he built us a new house, a little bungalow. He built it where the barn had previously stood. It was from the window of the new house that I watched the accident. Eventually, my brother Billy put a trailer beside our house, which he and his wife, Aloyse, lived in for years. Then on the other side of Billy's trailer, my brother Sidney built a house. By then he was married to Ginette and they had their daughter, Tanya. The bike shop that my dad and brothers started was in the front yard between the old house and the new one. Daddy used to store some of his bikes and snowmobiles in the old house.

Our little house was very simple, with a very small kitchen, a tiny dining room and a living room, and then a tiny little round hallway, off of which were the three bedrooms and bathroom. Nothing matched in that house. There was green industrial carpet in the bedrooms because they found it on sale, and there was a red shag carpet in the living room because that, too, was on sale, and they were able to find some red brocade curtains to match it. I loved those curtains, though my mother couldn't wait to be able to afford something better. My parents painted the walls themselves. I remember they painted the kitchen yellow and the bathroom pink, and since Sidney and Baby Guy were going to be living with us for a short time in that house, the room that they shared was painted half yellow and half purple. Guy wanted purple and Sidney wanted yellow. It's olive now, but if you pull the baseboards off in that room, you can still see a little bit of the remnants of that paint. My room, like the bathroom, was pink.

Most of my friends had houses far bigger and far grander than ours. But I can't tell you how proud and grateful Daddy was for that house. We would be sitting in the living room watching *The Fifth Estate* (which we did together my whole life), and he'd look over at me and say, "Aren't we lucky? We have this warm, comfortable house and there is food in the fridge. Every morning, I get a glass of ice-cold clean water from our tap and then take an orange out of the fridge. And I enjoy that looking out over this land. We are so lucky."

For Daddy, the comfort of a safe house, a clean glass of water and the financial wherewithal to eat an orange every day made him feel like a king. Every time he said this to me, I would roll my eyes. Like most teenagers, I had my head up my ass. I thought I was so much smarter than him because I'd never be satisfied with just that. All these years later, however, having taken on big debt to buy bigger and bigger houses, having squandered a fortune on things that I thought would make me happy, I realize my father was smarter than I will ever be. These days, I try to channel his attitude of gratitude. Someday, I would like an orange and a glass of water to make me feel the way they did for him.

As a young child, I wasn't really clear about our racial identity. My father had very dark skin. And I knew there were people on the reserve who we were related to. There was Uncle Mike and Aunt Margaret. Mike LaBillois was actually my father's cousin, and his wife, Margaret, went on to become the first woman chief in New Brunswick and was among the first Indigenous women in Canada to become a nurse. Back then, however, she was just Aunt Margaret to me. Later we came to find, as I mentioned, that she was my father's half-sister.

I remember visiting them at their house on the reserve. I also remember visiting the house of their daughter, May. I always thought May was so beautiful. She had long, black hair parted down the middle, beautiful mahogany skin and sparkly eyes that made it seem like she always had a really good secret. Her partner's name was Bruno. My father had some strict ideas about people living together out of wedlock. Somewhere along the way, it was explained to me that they were not married because May would not be allowed to live on the reserve if she married him. She would no longer be an Indian. I didn't fully understand the whole idea back then, but that was the only time I remember Daddy being okay with a non-married couple living together.

Aunt Margaret had lots of kids, fourteen I think, but May was the only one I knew as a child. She had a daughter named Sasha who was a few years younger than me. Sasha, whom I remember running around in her nightgown, has followed in her grandmother's footsteps and is now Chief at Eel River Bar.

At some point, shortly after I started school, we stopped going to the reserve. I attended a Catholic public school and used to get teased a lot. I was called Half-breed or spear chucker, but I struggled to understand who or what exactly I was. When that school closed down, my parents sent me to another Catholic elementary school for both French and English kids. I met other Indigenous kids my age for the first time. They lived on the reserve, and I knew that my parents and older brothers and sisters knew their families. We hung around at school, but I never went to their houses, nor they to mine. As I reflect on that now, I wonder if our absence from the reserve had something to do with my father's internalized racism.

During his childhood, Daddy was ostracized by the people in town. He was made to feel less than, and he never got past that. It had a long-lasting impact that made him always feel inferior. He attributed all my achievements to the fact that my mother was white. I know he was far more lenient with me than he was with my siblings, but there were certain things he was strict about. Me going to the reserve was one of those things. I lived in a drug- and alcohol-free house, and he didn't want me exposed to that elsewhere. It never dawned on him that those "nice," white homes I was going to had their own share of problems.

When I was about ten, we became involved in the New Brunswick Aboriginal Peoples Council. That was when I first heard the term "non-status Indian." Finally, I knew what I was. That clarity didn't last long because a few years later, the government classified anyone mixed race as being Métis. Oh, the poor Métis people. That causes confusion to this day. The Métis people are a separate group with their own culture, language and history. Eventually we went back to being non-status. All that changed starting with Bill C-31 in 1985. Now I am a status Indian, but who knows what label the government will come up with in the future to define me. Personally, however, I began to fully understand my own identity around the age of nineteen, so more on that in the chapters that follow.

Before I went to school, it was just me and my mom, together all the time up on the mountain, and I loved it. She was my favourite person on earth and remained so until the day she died. My wife understands when I tell people that my mother was the love of my life. I know no one will ever love me the way she did.

In the summers when I asked to have a picnic, she would make ham sandwiches on white bread, which she would wrap in wax paper and then tie into one of my dad's red-and-white polka-dot hankies, and she would pour some lemonade in a thermos. She would spread a blanket out on the grass just outside our dining room window and we would have our picnic. We read together and made puzzles together. She always made sure I had creative things to do, like string art or wood burning or beading. I often coloured while she either knitted or sewed. In most of the pictures of me in my childhood, I am wearing clothes that she made for me. And most of my dolls had clothes that she knit for them as well. My sister Sharron lived at home with us until I was ten. At that time, she was twenty and had joined the military. Sharron wasn't around much, and she and I didn't get along well at all until I was in my thirties, so my memories of those early summers were just me and Mommy.

Winter and summer, watching sports, both live and on TV, was something I did with my parents all the time. We never missed *The Wild World of Sports* on Saturday and Sunday nights, and we were big Expos fans. *Hockey Night in Canada* was practically a national holiday in our house, especially if our beloved Montreal Canadiens were playing. In fact, I took my first steps in our old house when the Canadiens scored a goal. Everyone was so excited. My mother theorized that I was not impressed with all the attention being paid to the Habs, so I stood up and walked to my father. My other major *Hockey Night in Canada* memory was not as pleasant. It was a treat my whole family loved, the smell of which made me sick to my stomach. During the first intermission, my mother would come in with a huge plate of sardine sandwiches. Let me explain said sandwiches. We are talking two slabs of my mom's homemade bread (that part was great) filled with a concoction of canned sardines, raw onion and mustard all mushed together. My family dove into those like it was foie gras at the Four Seasons!

Before the era of twenty-four-hour sports channels, televised sport was a big deal and we never missed the Olympics or our favourite teams. Habs all winter and Expos all summer! The one thing Mommy watched that Daddy and I couldn't get into was golf. I found it boring to watch. Daddy used to say to her, "Woman, you've got champagne taste on a beer income."

I don't think I knew what a beer income was, but I knew we weren't "rich" like my friends. The people I thought were rich when I was a child were actually just middle class, with the exception of a couple of them whose families really did have serious quid. I never thought of us as poor, though. I knew my dad had been poor as a child, and I had never been hungry so I figured we were just fine. Although I do remember when filling out my student loan application, I had to document my family income. When I asked my parents, they said, $16,000 per year. Even by 1986 standards, that was not very much. I looked at the chart in the student loan booklet and that income was listed as poverty line. I thought there must be a mistake. I clarified with my parents and told them what the chart said. My father asked me, "Have you ever felt poor?" "No," I replied. To which Daddy responded, "Then don't worry about what the chart says." Like I said, he was way smarter than I will ever be.

My dad was different from other dads in the way he earned a living. In the first few years of my life, Daddy worked in the paper mill, but we also had this bike shop in the yard. Then at some point, he quit his job in the mill, and for my school years, he and my brother Sidney ran the shop, which was a Harley-Davidson dealership. Later, my brother Billy joined them. Daddy was the boss, Sidney was the head mechanic and my brother Billy was an artist and did custom paint jobs on the bikes. I was used to always having long-haired guys in leather around. They used to bring me little things from time to time, and I had crushes on a different biker every week. Daddy kept a close eye on me, however, as he didn't want me growing up to hang out with the bikers . . . customers or not!

Every day when I walked up the hill after school, my dad and brothers would be in the yard and my mom in the house waiting for me. I have never ever had a key to my house because there was never a time when I would come home to an empty house.

Before going to school, the only friends I had were Connie and Denise Frenette. They lived at the bottom of the hill, and when I was about four, my sister Sharron started babysitting them and their brother and older sister. So Sharron made my first friends for me. We skied together and theirs was the first house at which I had sleepovers. Their mother, Beulah Frenette, had a big impact on me. They built a new house a few kilometres up the road, which to this day is my favourite house I have ever been in. I still have low-key fantasies of either building a replica of the Frenette home or buying the original as a vacation spot. As we aged and I got into sports, the Frenette girls and I drifted apart, but I am still thrilled when I see them and still hold tight to the wonderful memories of my first friendships.

My oldest brother, Billy, was the leader of our family. He was born about a year after my mom and dad were married. The first-born and a boy, he had a lot of my dad's personality, and from a very young age, he took on the role of the leader. I'm going to tell you about Billy, starting with my own memories, but as an adult, long after Billy died, I found out so many things I didn't know about when he was living.

When I was born, Billy was twenty-one, and he had already met his wife. They got married the year I was born. People wonder why I am so close to my sister-in-law—well, Aloyse has been in my family longer than I have! They didn't have children for eight years after they got married, so all my early memories of Billy are always Billy and Aloyse . . . and me! They were newlyweds but they couldn't shake me. I did everything with them.

He was a great athlete, an incredible skier. He got me my first pair of skis when I was four. And I had these gorgeous blue-glitter ski boots that he bought me, and a red bomber jacket, and these "stretchies" that I would wear, and a Spider Sabich ski hat (a hand-me-down from Billy). I was all decked out in my outfit along with my ski glasses and no front teeth. I was all ready for my ski lesson. Billy was a big man. He later owned a bodybuilding gym and he worked out all his life, but he was naturally big to begin with, very muscular. So there I was ready for my ski lesson when he leaned over and put his hand on my chest, and poof! He pushed me down into the snow. I said, "I thought you were going to teach me how to ski." He said, "Oh, I'm going to teach you how to ski, but first I'm going to teach you how to get up, because falling is inevitable when you're learning how to ski. But once you know how to get up, then you'll ski without fear." When I was four, I thought he was talking to me about skiing. Twenty-five years after his death, I realized he was giving me one of his greatest life lessons. I live my life without fear because I know how to get up.

It wasn't just skiing that we did together. I remember him teaching me how to play baseball because he was a great baseball player. He'd played for the town team, the Dalhousie Dodgers. He bought me a navy-blue Louisville Slugger, which I still have. And years later, when I was cast in *Trailer Park Boys*, they had me wielding a gun in the script, and I asked if I could bring my own weapon. I showed up on set with a hot-pink Louisville Slugger instead. To me, it paid a bit of homage to Billy as well.

But before I got the navy Louisville Slugger, Billy had a little two-by-two stick for me. We were in the backyard, and I had a tennis ball. He was just tossing the tennis ball to me underhand, and I was holding the stick as if it were a bat and swinging away. I'd mostly swing and miss, have a hard time connecting with the ball. It took me a while to figure out I had to look at the ball and not where I wanted the ball to go. It was a beautiful summer night. Summer nights on the Palmater compound are the very best of summer nights! The east wind was blowing, keeping the bugs at bay. The sun was setting, lighting up the mountains on the Gaspé coast and sparkling off the Baie des Chaleur. Just another beautiful night at home.

There I am, swinging away. Standing just above us is my mom in her housedress, taking some clothes in off the line, which was a pretty common summer occurrence. My mom was in her early forties when she had me, with a full head of grey hair. I always knew she was strong, but I saw her as an "older woman." She was the age of most of my friends' grandparents. When you're young and your parents are that much older, you don't think about who they were when they were young. I thought that Billy and I were the big athletes of the family, that nobody else in our family could understand what he and I shared.

Mommy finished taking the clothes off the line and she had her clothes basket wedged between her right hip and her right arm, as she always carried it. She was slowly sashaying toward the house with the east wind blowing her dress up against her legs. And what a pair of legs they were. She had great legs well into her seventies. As she walked across the back veranda to go into the house with the clothes, Billy said to me, "You should hand that stick to Mommy—she'll show you how to hit a ball." I laughed because I thought he was kidding. And when I laughed, Billy and Mommy shared a look. Something passed between them. She dropped the clothes basket right where she was standing, stepped down off the veranda and put her hand out for me to hand her the stick. When I handed it to her, she said, "This is too small to choke up on. I don't think I will be able to get much torque." Without warning, Billy tossed that tennis ball at her, and she nailed it. It flew so far and fast I couldn't whip my head around quick enough to see where it landed in the back field. When I looked toward her, she had the clothes basket tucked against her hip and she was disappearing through the back door of the house. I looked at Billy and he just smiled at me. I spent the rest of that evening trying to find that tennis ball. When I found it, there was a split in the seam of it. She had hit it so hard with the corner of that stick that it split the ball. That was a defining moment for me. It was the first time I realized that my mother had once been young. Might she, too, have had dreams? And might some of those dreams been left unanswered?

I then got really curious about her young life and started asking questions. She dug out a picture she was proud to show me. It was her at the starting line of the Dalhousie Married Women's Race. It was sponsored by the local newspaper. I'm not sure if it was part of our summer festival or not, but it was a running race for the married women in town. She looked at it, the corners of her mouth just hinting at a smile. As she ran her fingers over the picture, she said, "I won. I won every year." Later, when we would watch the Olympics together, she would always say to my dad and me, "I think I could have been a runner." Daddy would say, "You were a runner." But I knew what she meant. She did have dreams. Some answered. Some left wanting.

I realized that day with the split ball that my brother Billy knew my mother in a different way than I did. Billy grew up with Mommy. She was only nineteen when she had him. His experience of my mother was completely different from my experience of her, because she was so mature and wise and had figured out motherhood by the time I came along. But Billy was her first, and I think they learned a lot together. I know they shared a lot. When Billy died at the age of fifty, he took a part of her with him. I could see my father's emotional scars but I could never see my mother's scars. She was so strong. It seemed like nothing ever shook her. But when Billy died, it brought my mother to her knees. She told me later, "The only reason I was able to get back out of bed was because I had five kids left." Billy's death changed her. Billy's death changed us all.

But I'm getting ahead of myself. Let me go back to my early years with Billy. Once I learned how to ski, Billy and Aloyse would buy my ski pass for me every winter. This was an expensive pass that gave me unlimited access to the local ski hill all season long. Without it, I could never have done all that skiing as a kid. Winter is my favourite season and the love of skiing as a child has a lot to do with that. Every single weekend, I would ski with them. In the evenings, when they would come home with pizza or Dixie Lee chicken, out my back door and into their trailer I would go. I didn't knock. I would just plow through the door. "Oh, you're having pizza! I'm here to have pizza too!" When I think back on it now, here they were, a young couple in their early twenties, and I was with them constantly. People in town sometimes made the mistake of thinking they were my parents and that Mommy and Daddy were my grandparents. Though he was my brother and my godfather, in a lot of ways, he was like another father to me.

He was also like a second husband to my mother, because my dad and my mom did not have a lot in common. All the things she loved to do, like shopping, fall fairs, summer festivals and parades, were things that Daddy loathed. I used to think it was just a matter of personal taste, and I also thought he was just being ornery and hard to get along with. Now that I suffer from the same condition he suffered from, advanced osteoarthritis, I have a different perspective. Either way, as a woman living out of town without a driver's licence, Mommy might have missed out on so much, but Billy took her to all those things. If there was a parade in town, Billy would take Mom and me with him and Aloyse. When there were things happening at the rink, or anything happening that we would want to go to, or even if we wanted to go to the mall, go shopping, it was Billy, Aloyse, Mommy and me.

Eight years later, Billy and Aloyse had their first child. Everyone thought that I was going to be extremely jealous when this child came along, but in fact, when their daughter, Vicky, was born, I thought they had her just for me. I saw her as my own little doll, and I used to dress her up, put makeup on her, do her hair, take pictures of her. We were aunt and niece, but we grew up a lot like sisters. She slept at my house all the time.

Billy played in the first international tattoo back when he was in the navy. When I was born, he was aboard the naval ship the *Saguenay*. All the sailors on board had been taking bets on when I would be born, whether I'd be a boy or a girl, and how much I would weigh. They were having a big party on the ship when the telegram arrived announcing my birth. Billy jumped on the stage and took the microphone from the band for a minute to announce that at three o'clock that afternoon, his new baby sister came into the world at ten pounds, fifteen and a half ounces. Whenever I am on radio or TV, I wonder if any of those sailors, in their seventies now, realize I'm that baby they bet on back in 1968.

Billy was the oldest and he died so young, so I tend to talk about him a lot, but there is a whole cast of supporting characters in the story of my life. Each of them has given me special gifts that have helped me on my way. I've shared laughs and tears with all of them. Let me introduce you to some of them now. . . .

The one where siblings act like siblings and Christmas is almost cancelled

Sixteen months after Billy was born, my brother Sidney was born at home. As I mentioned earlier, I was just short of eleven pounds at birth, but my mother swears that Sidney was even bigger. He was never weighed because it was a home birth, but she was sure, and since she was the one who did the hard work of bringing us both into this world, I tend to believe her. When you look at baby pictures of my whole family (well, there are no baby pictures of Sharron but more on that later), you cannot tell the difference between Sidney and me. We both look like the same really big Inuit baby. Neither of us look Inuit as adults but we sure did look that way as infants.

My mother often said, "Sidney is the only one of my kids that turned out like me." She was right. He has a lot of my mother's traits. He was twenty when I was born and we are very close. We were very close in my first four years, before Billy started getting me into skiing. He used to work on the motorcycles while sitting on a little stool next to the bike. I would come outside in my little red splash suit, get between him and the bike and lay against him. He never shooed me away; he would go right on working with an arm on either side of me. After Billy died, Sidney and I became even closer. All three of my brothers have this unique quality of being big, strong men's men, but also very sweet, kind people. That set the bar pretty high for me when it came to looking for a man to measure up.

If I described Billy as the archetype of a jock, then I would describe Sidney as a bad boy. He looked a lot like Charles Bronson in his younger years. His hair was long and he always had a moustache. At seventy, that is still true, but now the hair, thinning on top, is always brought into a neat braid at the back of his head. He was wild when he was young. There are so many stories of bike and car crashes, one elbow burnt to the bone on the pavement after a motorcycle accident, front teeth knocked out after a car accident. Women, wine and weed played a big part in his young life. He was also running with some bad cats and did a short stint in jail. To me, however, he was just my big, sweet brother who never seemed bothered by my constant presence.

When I was four, a woman came along and took him from me. That woman was Ginette, now his wife of forty-five years. We laugh at it now, but at the time, I was so jealous of her. Because Billy and Sidney were always on the compound, they were the two siblings I was closest to most of my life. Billy met his wife before I was born so I always knew Billy with Aloyse, but Sidney was all mine until Ginette came along, and that took some time for me to get over. When they got married, I was the flower girl at their wedding. Ginette was a school-teacher, and years later she would bring me to school with her in the last week of summer when she was getting ready for the coming year. She taught grade three in the French school in Eel River Crossing. I loved it! We would decorate her class-room and prepare name tags. She would have me photocopy, which thrilled me. If you are thinking of the typical modern Xerox machine, you are probably wondering why I would find that exciting. The photocopying I was doing, however, was on a machine that had a big circular drum covered in carbon and involved cranking it the way you would an old pencil sharpener to make your copies one at a time. Kind of prehistoric, but so awesome for ten-year-old me.

Once Sidney got married, he wasn't around as much, but he and I always had a special bond. He is naturally gifted as a mechanic. He is curious and has an open mind. I can talk to him for hours. The only time I've ever fished in my life was with him. I loved going with him. It wasn't about the fishing; it was about the time alone with him.

Sidney and Billy were very close all their lives. I know Billy's death really impacted him. Sidney's own son died of cancer at the age of twenty-five, a few years after Billy died, but like my mom, he was resilient through both losses. He kept my parents emotionally afloat through it all.

Sidney, like Mommy, doesn't like conflict. He does not argue. He doesn't always think he is right. That was a special trait of both Billy and me. He was never at the centre of the yelling matches at our family gatherings. We had a tradition on the mountain on Christmas mornings. My dad slept in, while my mom and I got up and opened our gifts. We would then go over to Billy's house and get them up (they were late sleepers) and watch Vicky and their son, James, open their gifts. Then all of us would head over to Sidney's place (they were early risers), where the kids, Tanya and Jonathan, had already opened their gifts. Sidney would prepare a bacon and egg breakfast for all of us, and by then Daddy would be up and would come over for the breakfast. This was always my mother's favourite part of Christmas Day. She could relax and enjoy herself before the hard work of preparing Christmas dinner for twenty-five people started.

Christmas Eve, the whole family would go to Mass, and then we usually got together at someone's house. One year, we celebrated Christmas Eve at my brother Baby Guy's house. The whole family was there and we were all enjoying ourselves. The sisters-in-law were the quietest among us and usually making tea. The kids were running around. Everyone was in a state of merriment. My father, Billy and Sidney were sitting at the round table in Guy's kitchen. The boys were having a few drinks, and a discussion started about a snowmobile. Sidney, the mechanic, gave his opinion, and Billy, the non-mechanic, argued with him. We all loved Billy but we also knew that he always thought he was right and he had a tendency to raise his voice to prove his point, often with some spit flying while he did it.

I'd seen arguments like this a thousand times. A thousand times, Sidney would just let it go, even if he knew he was right. On that night, however, Sidney had been drinking rye and just wasn't in the mood for it. He engaged in the argument. It escalated fast. Then my father, always one to throw gasoline on a raging fire, got in on it and took Sidney's side. Suddenly the chairs are toppled over backwards and both boys are on their feet. Everyone else in the house got very quiet as Sidney suggested they go outside to settle the matter. I can see it in my mind's eye like it was yesterday. My brother Guy, bigger than both of them, was trying to keep them separated, while my sisters-in-law, both so much shorter, were trying to get the attention of their respective husbands. Guy finally managed to separate them, and the party quickly dispersed, with the kids asking if Christmas was cancelled.

The next morning Mommy and I got up with heavy hearts. What would Christmas morning be without our traditions? We opened some of our gifts but our hearts were not into it. We sat down at our dining room table, which has a big picture window looking out on our yard and Billy's house. We both had our head in our hands, elbows on the table, worried faces. Then we saw it. Billy's front door opened. Out came Billy. He was wearing the old, ratty blue housecoat that he always wore. His bare legs were exposed, and he had on a pair of skidoo boots. In his hands was a hockey stick with a white sheet tied to it. He crunched down his snow-covered steps and started walking toward Sidney's house, which was on the other side of ours.

Without a word exchanged between us, Mommy and I jumped up and ran out into the sun porch, which gave us a clear view to Sidney's house. Sidney's house was a split-level. The door was at ground level and the living room picture window sits about six feet off the ground. Mommy and I had our faces pushed to our window as we watched Billy make his way to the front of Sid's house. He raised the hockey stick up and knocked on the window with it. We waited as he waited. Sidney came to the window and Billy waved the white sheet back and forth. After a one-minute lapse while we all held our breath, the front door opened. Sidney stepped out and the two men hugged. My heart soared and Mommy yelled, "Get your coat! Christmas is back on!!"

That was the nature of their relationship. Billy was quick to apologize and Sidney was quick to forgive. Sidney continues to be a sort of peacekeeper in our family. He calls us all on special occasions. If any of us are having a hard time, he is the one who checks on us. When my dad was in the old people's home, Sidney visited him every day and called him after supper every night. He is the strong, silent type. It is hard to get him to open up and talk about his own hard times. He has a positive outlook on life. He has a wonderful relationship with his wife. It seems cliché, but she really is his best friend. They love to go in the woods together, the place where he is happiest. They still shower together after forty-five years of marriage and I don't mean that in a sexual way. They are just so close that they take their shower together every morning. He shares many stories with me of times past, but I know he keeps even more to himself. Those still waters run deep.

The next in line in our family is Penny, the first-born girl. God help her! Being the first girl in a house with a misogynist father who was still drinking wasn't easy. In many ways, it was like she was given the responsibility of breaking trail for Sharron and me, but she didn't have the disposition for it. Penny made a lot of bad decisions, but she was the kindest person and accepted everyone for who they were. She never wanted more from people than they were capable of giving. I wish I had more of that part of her in me. Penny was never good at navigating rough waters. She rebelled against my parents' values and was impregnated at nineteen by her best friend's father. When her son came, I was thrilled. At four years old, I had another kid in the family for the first time. I have a beautiful picture of the two of us sitting in a cardboard box in our kitchen. She kept Jason for a year. Penny was struggling with addiction to drugs and alcohol, and so when he was one, she gave him to a family in town through a private adoption. My mom wanted to take him, but she was in her late forties with a five-year-old of her own. She was also worried that my father would favour me over Jason, and that it would have a negative effect on him. There was talk of Billy and Aloyse taking him, but then Penny mentioned getting him back once he was older. My mother thought this would cause problems down the road and had the potential to rip the family apart. So in the end, our beautiful little Jason was given to a family in town, who changed his name. I was so confused. I remember my mom telling me that he was no longer going to be in our family, that he was no longer going to be the name I knew him as and that I had to be careful how I addressed him when I saw him around town. I remember visiting him once at the trailer where he lived downtown, and after that, the only time I saw him was by happenstance in town.

A few years later, Penny was pregnant again, and this time she gave the boy up for adoption at birth. My mom and I often spoke about our two lost boys. When I was really young, I asked her how Penny could give them away. My mom said, "I don't know, baby, I could never give my children away so I can't explain it to you."

Fourteen years later, he found us. He was adopted by a wonderful couple who couldn't have kids. Once they adopted him, they got pregnant and had another boy. They all came to visit us, and I took my long-lost nephew for a drive, just he and I. He looked more Indigenous than the other grandkids and he was quiet. His mouth and dimples were very similar to mine. I cherish that hour with him. We never saw him again.

His adopted family had told him he was given away because Penny couldn't care for him. When he arrived and saw all the grandkids running around the compound and all the houses and cars, he couldn't understand why there was no room in all of them for him. His mother wrote my mother a letter explaining that he was in therapy and did not want further contact with us. Penny's older son became an engineer, married with three kids. He has also cut off contact with our family.

I think of them both often. I think of them as our lost boys. My heart aches and breaks for them. I wonder who they are as men. Do they look like me? Do they ever see me on TV? And if they do, do they think of me as their aunt? I think of them as my nephews and worry about their happiness. Ultimately, I respect their wishes, but I would be so thrilled to be able to hug them just once more before I die.

Years later Penny got clean and sober. She was almost thirty years sober at the time of her death. All my childhood, she was like a myth to me.

She was like a myth because she did all the things that I would be scared to death to do. She smoked, she drank, she had sex with men who weren't her husband, and I didn't know how she did that while sharing the same father with me. I was always scared to death of Daddy's disapproval or of falling from his grace. Penny was not. She and he had a very strained relationship. They were alike in so many ways. They would both vehemently deny that, but I think the rest of us all recognized it and knew that it was a big part of why they butted heads.

Since she wasn't around much, I would get so excited when I knew she was going to come to visit. If we expected her on a Saturday, I would look forward to it all week. Sometimes she showed. Sometimes she didn't. But when I was with her, she always made me feel great about myself. When I thought I was ugly, she thought I was beautiful. When I said I wanted to be a writer, she said I could be. When I said I wanted to be a rock star, she said I could be. She was a dreamer, like me. But while she believed in me, she never figured out the next step for herself, all the hard work that had to follow the dream to make it happen. She was always stuck in the dreaming part. She could sing and would often sing in local bars . . . usually Patsy Cline songs. Although she dreamed about a music career a lot, she never pursued it.

Penny was a bartender for years and then held odd jobs around town. She eventually went on old age pension. Penny met a woman named Yoland when she was around the same age I was when I met my wife, Denise. They were together for thirty years. Penny lived her whole life in Dalhousie. She made all her mistakes and all her bad choices right there in that little town. You would have a hard time finding anyone in that town who didn't love her, though. She was kind. She never held a grudge. No matter how hard up she was, she couldn't walk by a person in need without offering whatever might be in her pocket.

A few years back, I was leaving town after a visit and stopped at the Irving to gas up for the road. A woman I did not know stopped me. She recognized me. We chatted for a few moments. I was trying to refer to a person whose last name had skipped my mind. I said to her, "You know, she is my sister Penny's friend." The woman smiled at me and said, "That doesn't narrow it down. Everyone is Penny's friend." That made this little sister very proud.

When I got the deal for this book, Penny was so proud, and she asked me often how close I was to finishing it. As I was working on the final edits, she broke a hip. In the three years or so leading up to that point, Penny had lost her will to live and she spent most of her time in a La-Z-Boy in her living room, trying to chase away the ghosts in her head. I was often impatient with her inability to shake it off. After her hip surgery, she never got out of the hospital bed. It had been almost two years since I had seen her due to the Covid-19 lockdown. Four months after the hip surgery, she died in that hospital bed at the age of seventy-one.

I was in the middle of a virtual keynote from my bedroom in Toronto when she passed. My final words in my keynote were "Please remember you are enough. Love yourself." When Denise came into the room, I knew by the look on her face that Penny was gone. I wish Penny could have heard those words. If only she could have loved herself as much as she loved me, she would have had a different life. It has reinforced for me the importance of self-acceptance and self-kindness. I have now witnessed, first-hand, that it is a matter of life and death.

Penny was too fragile for this life. She never got the chance to read this book, but I hope she knew how much I loved her.

Next came my brother Guy. I think if he was born decades later, he would have been diagnosed with ADHD and hyperactivity. Back then, everyone just thought he was bad. His older brothers teased him relentlessly. He wanted my father's love, but Daddy was always so much harder on him than he was on the older two. Daddy and his drinking buddies would also tease and torment Guy relentlessly. He had a number of really bad accidents as a kid. On his first day of school, he was hit by a car and ended up in a coma in the hospital. No one can remember how long he was in the coma, but his head was badly injured and my parents were told he might not make it. Another time, he was in the cab of a truck going down a steep hill in town, and when the truck made a left-hand turn, the door opened and Guy fell out of the moving truck into the road. Yet another time, he was riding his bike as fast as he could down a hill and across a street. Just as he came to the street at full speed, a large town works truck appeared. Guy slammed into the side of it . . . back to the hospital he went. Mommy used to tell me she was worried the people at the hospital thought she was abusing him because he was so accident-prone.

One other aspect of Guy's childhood always sat heavy on my mother's heart. When he was twelve years old, he was caught stealing some candy at a local store. The police brought him home. My father wasn't there. They told my timid mother that she had a choice: they were either going to bring him to jail or to "the Provincial." The Provincial is our colloquial term for the mental hospital located in Campbellton. Mommy didn't know any of her rights and she didn't want her twelve-year-old going to jail. Without Daddy there, she had to make the decision on her own. She chose the Provincial. They kept him for two weeks and gave him multiple rounds of electroshock therapy. That left emotional scars on both Guy and Mommy.

Guy and Sidney got married in the same year. When Guy married Donna, my father did not attend the wedding. He skipped it for the most ridiculous reason. The couple didn't have much money at all, so my father told him they could spend their wedding night in my mom and dad's room. Guy insisted on getting a hotel. (As he should have. Can you imagine spending your wedding night in your parents' bed?) As a result, Daddy refused to go to the wedding. In some ways, I think Daddy skipped the wedding just to hurt Guy. I could never figure out why Daddy was so cruel to him. Years later, Daddy would insist he had gone to the wedding. We would show him the pictures and point out that he was not in any of them. But he insisted he was there. He wasn't. It was another disappointment for Guy in a lifetime of disappointments. Guy and Donna had two children, Roxanne and Derek, and when the kids were young, they had some hard times because work was hard to find in Dalhousie. Guy has a strong work ethic, however, and he was strong and would do anything to support his family. He is now sixty-seven and is supposed to be retired. He has a beautiful house, which he paid off long ago. He is financially secure and spoils his grandsons, but he is still work-ing. He is working on the reserve as what in a municipality you might call the manager of public works. He also has a small engine business in the garage in his backyard.

One of the jobs he used to do around town when he was younger was working security at dances. What we called "bouncing." He was the bouncer at all my high school dances. I couldn't have gotten pregnant in high school if I tried! He was big and kind-hearted. Everyone loved him, but they took him seriously. He wasn't a bully. If he needed to bounce someone, he would discreetly tell them they had to go and would give them the opportunity to leave voluntarily with their dignity intact. There were times when people mistook his kind nature. I've seen him throw a guy out of a dance and into a snowbank up to his waist, just as though he were throwing a spear.

One year I went to the Halloween dance dressed as a can of Alpine beer. My friend Mark went dressed as a shower. He had a round hoop rigged up over his head with a shower curtain fully enclosing him. He was wearing boxer shorts and a shower cap. Before going to the dance, he suggested I hide the beer inside my can costume, assuming my brother would not pat me down. We got in without incident. We were on the dance floor sneaking sips of beer inside the shower curtain when sud-denly Guy whipped open the curtain and said, "Wait until I tell Daddy!" I thought I was going to pass out. The idea of my father finding out I was drinking at the age of sixteen was more than I could bear. Guy let a beat drop and then finished his sentence: ". . . that you are in the shower with a boy! Ha ha ha." He walked off laughing. I think it took ten full minutes before either Mark or I got our breathing back to normal.

Guy and I were never as close as I was with my other brothers, although I knew he would destroy anyone who touched a hair on my head. When I was about thirty-four, he and his wife, Donna, came to Halifax to visit me and Denise. It was the first time we really talked. Over three days, he shared a lot of his feelings and memories with me and said he always saw me as a sort of alien because the life I led was so different from his. All the love that was showered on me as a child seemed to him so different. He did not have that sense of love and protection growing up.

It hasn't affected who he is as a man. He is a wonderful grandfather. He is kind and has a sweet innocence to him that lets you see a glimpse of the boy he once was. He is big and sweet and just a bit damaged by his early life.

After Guy, my brother Bruce was born, as I described. There is not much more to say about Bruce. I never knew him. He died at three months old, but his brief existence, according to my mother, is the reason my father got sober. So I always say I am the youngest of seven, not six, because even though I never knew him, Bruce was my brother and I love him.

The last to be born before me was Sharron. My relationship with Sharron is the most complicated of all my sibling relationships. Sharron was the baby for eleven years before I came along. Although she was born in 1958 and me in 1968, her birthday is in February and mine is in December, so she is close to eleven years older than me. Sharron arrived at a tough time. She was born the year my father got sober. Anyone who has ever been a serious alcoholic will know that the months following your last drink are very hard. All the messes and mistakes you made, which had been hidden in a fog of booze, have to be faced and dealt with. Money was extremely tight at that time. One small way that this affected Sharron is that there was no money to buy or develop film. As a result, there is a plethora of pictures of the five of us as babies and even a couple of Bruce as a baby, but there are absolutely no pictures of Sharron as a baby. There was one picture of her at about four or five years old, but she gave it to the yearbook committee at school the year she graduated and it was lost. I think that is the perfect metaphor for Sharron's life. I think she always felt a little bit invisible, which she may have had in common with my mom. She went to school when people still remembered Daddy as an alcoholic, and the people she was in school with knew about our sister Penny's antics. All this weighed on her.

When life finally started getting good at age eleven, along came me. She was no longer the baby. And even when she was the baby, she didn't get babied the way I did. She loved me, but I think she also wished I had never been born.

One winter day, when I was three or four, my mom asked, in the middle of the afternoon, if I wanted a drumstick for supper. I was so stoked! A drumstick for supper! Yahoo. When I sat down at the dinner table, my mother put a chicken leg on my plate. A chicken leg? "What is this?" I asked her. She told me it was a drumstick. I promptly informed her that it was not a drumstick and that drumsticks are made of ice cream and have nuts on top of them and she had promised me one! A crying jag followed until finally my father said, "Sharron, get dressed and walk down the hill to Mrs. Scott's canteen and get the baby a drumstick." Out into the cold she went. That pretty much set the stage for the twenty-seven or so years that followed. There were many incidents between us that stick out. There was an event that involved her holding the rope to the sled I was on and "accidentally" letting it go, shooting me down the hill toward the road at breakneck speed. She swears it was an accident. She slammed my hand in a door twice! Once in the basement door and once in the bathroom door. Both times, I was running after her; both times I lost the fingernail on my middle finger as a result.

As soon as my "big" teeth came in, she started calling me Bucky Beaver. She continually and relentless told me I had buckteeth. If you have ever seen me or a picture of me, you will know that I have beautiful, straight teeth. You could not convince me of that in my teens. I begged my dentist for braces. At every visit, I would ask for them. Sharron was an adult by then and I was pubescent with all the insecurities that come with puberty. There is even a school picture where I smiled with my mouth closed for fear that others would notice how buck my teeth were. I was convinced I was ugly and that my teeth were a big part of it.

At eighteen, I saw a new dentist and he asked me who had done my orthodontic work. After some confusion on my part, he told me that my teeth were so nice and straight, he assumed I had braces at some point. I'd had many compliments on my teeth by then, but that dentist was the first person I believed. Finally, the myth of my buckteeth was released. Years later, Sharron was present when someone complimented my teeth. I looked at her. She laughed and said to the person, "I called her Bucky Beaver when she was growing up because she had nice teeth and I had a big gap between my front teeth. I was just jealous." She laughed and the conversation carried on. There was my explanation.

As you can see, when Sharron was still at home, our relationship was horrible. I remember being at a wedding and the bride tossing the bouquet in my direction. All the other single ladies backed up to let me catch the bouquet. I was only seven. Sharron was eighteen. When I caught the bouquet, she grabbed it with both hands and tore it to pieces. My father was furious at her. At the time, I couldn't figure out why she was so mean. I wasn't old enough to understand jealousy.

She joined the military when she was twenty, but even with her out of the house, our relationship continued to deteriorate. It was so complicated, though. At my birthday, she always got me the thing I wanted most. I wanted high-top leather Converse basketball sneakers (no one else at my school had them), and she got them for me. When I wanted Levi's button-fly jeans, she got them for me. When I was fourteen and she was only twenty-five, her Christmas gift to me was a trip to Disney. She flew me to Florida where she and her husband, Bill, lived during the winter months, and for a week, she brought me to all the cool places kids love in Florida. Yet, we could barely be in the same room together at home without tearing one another apart.

It got to the point where my whole family was anxious when they knew we were both coming home at the same time. They knew there would be war. And yet, all that time, as frustrated as I was with our relationship, I knew if I ever really needed her, she would come take care of me. The couple of times I got in trouble financially in my twenties, I didn't call my parents for help. I called Sharron. I would ask her to keep it a secret. She would not. She made sure my parents and my whole family knew. She made sure I was humiliated by the entire experience . . . but she gave me the money.

One year was particularly bad. We weren't speaking at all. I was living in Halifax and working two jobs at once. I was sleep-deprived and my clothes were falling off me. Working day and night had resulted in a lot of weight loss, but I couldn't afford to buy new jeans, so I wore my old baggy jeans with a belt to keep them up. My birthday rolled around and an envelope arrived from Sharron with a gift certificate for Sears. I went and bought a new pair of jeans and a bottle of perfume. Like I said, it was complicated.

The year of the new millennium, what we all called Y2K, when everyone thought our modern banking system was going to crash, my father had a quadruple bypass just after Christmas. My sister and I both landed in Saint John to be with my mom and to be by his side for his surgery. Something happened on that trip and we bonded . . . finally. I think Mommy's joy at us getting along overshadowed her worry about Daddy.

Sharron and her husband now live in the house I grew up in. They came home to look after my mother for the last six years of her life. I go to visit often. I step as carefully as possible around Sharron. I think she does the same, but I think we both do it because the peace between us is worth the effort. We love one another fiercely. She is one of my biggest fans and I know she is proud of me. We are the only two girls left. We need one another. Every time something good used to happen to me, I would call my parents to tell them so they could share in the joy. Now when something good happens, I tell Sharron. She shares the joy with me. It's not the kind of sister relationship you see on TV where we like all the same things and do everything together. In fact, we are quite different, but I don't know what I would do without her. So, if your kids fight mercilessly, don't despair, there is hope.

So those are my siblings. They are the people who shaped my young life, but there was another group of people who added a whole lot of colour to my world: the bikers.

SCENE 4

The one where my dad tries to keep me away from the bikers

G rowing up in a motorcycle dealership is a very interesting experience. Growing up in a Harley-Davidson
dealership in the seventies was downright surreal.

My father always worked on bikes as a side hustle. He had a
lot of side hustles, everything from bootlegging to taxi driving,
but mechanics was always a mainstay. He would buy a busted
bike for fifty bucks, take it apart, clean every part and repair any
parts that were broken, then he would put it back together. He
could sell the restored bike for $200. My brother Sidney was
always by his side. At first he held the light as Daddy worked,

but slowly his own mechanical abilities developed. He is the definition of a gearhead. As I mentioned earlier, Sidney spent a short amount of time in jail when he was very young. He was running with the wrong crowd and my parents worried they were going to lose him to a life of crime. When he was in jail, my father thought that a motorcycle repair shop might give Sid something to focus on once he got out. My mother agreed, and thus Sid's cycle shop was born.

It always fascinated me how good Sidney was with mechanics, so I asked him once, "How did you get so good at it?" And he said, "I used to hand Daddy the tools." And I said, "Well, how did Daddy get so good at it?" And he said, "He used to hold the light for his brother, Frank." So, in a way, mechanics is a family legacy—for the men in my family, anyway. I certainly don't have any mechanical ability, although I do love bikes and bikers.

When Daddy had this idea, he thought Sid's repair shop would be just that, a repair shop. A man named Mr. Sullivan was closing his shop, and Daddy bought all of his tools and manuals. The land Daddy bought was originally a farm, so there was a barn and various other outbuildings. Sidney had his tools set up in a little shed just upslope from the original farmhouse. It was to that little shed I would run, with the legs of my splash suit making swishing sounds to let Sid know I was coming. At first, I think Sid loved the work. It was what interested him and he was good at it. My father was still employed in the mill, so Sidney did most of the work. In the beginning, they were repairing Jawas, Yamahas, BSAs and other smaller bikes. In the early seventies, Daddy and Sidney decided to get into the Harley-Davidson business. There were no Harley dealers in Atlantic Canada at that time, so they decided to give it a shot.

At that point, my father quit his job in the mill, and a big sign was erected halfway up our hill that read "Palmater's Cycle Shop." Just to be clear, for anyone who has wandered into a Harley-Davidson dealership in the last ten years, Harley-Davidsons in the early seventies were driven by bikers. It was not the popular, mid-life crisis bike for doctors and lawyers that it has become today. There were no fancy showrooms back then. The business moved out of the little shack and into one of the larger farm buildings located where my brother Billy's house is today. They constructed a ramp at the front door so the bikes could be rolled in and out.

Daddy and Sidney built a flatbed trailer they could haul behind our Ford F-150 truck (Daddy always had a Ford F-150 truck), and they headed for Montreal. My father had never liked the idea of credit. He was a man who figured that, in life, you should pay as you go. When I was in high school, I remember Mastercard calling him and informing him he had not used his credit card in a year and he needed to use it to keep it active. He went to the drugstore and bought a package of razor blades with his Mastercard and stopped at the bank to make a payment on the card in the amount of the blades. He always boasted that no credit card company would make a dime of interest on him! If only I had his restraint when it comes to credit cards!

Because of his aversion to credit, when Daddy and Sid travelled to Montreal, they did so with an envelope of cash. The first two Harleys they bought were for my brother Billy and a man named Paul Galloway. Daddy couldn't read or write very well at all. He would be considered illiterate by today's standards, having never attended even grade school, but he was smart enough not to get in hock to the Harley-Davidson Corporation. They would travel back to Montreal, buy bikes, come home and sell them, and then do it all over again. I'm not sure that anyone could operate a Harley dealership that way in this day and age. But my dad came along at just the right time and it worked. If you lived on the Gaspé coast of Quebec, New Brunswick or Nova Scotia and you bought a Harley-Davidson, you bought it from Palmater's Cycle Shop.

My father was paying Sidney ten dollars an hour as the primary mechanic, and Sidney was working around the clock. There was a constant parade of motorcycles and motorcycle drivers in and out of our yard. For the first ten years of my life, I thought my name was "Mother, take the baby in the house." I was fascinated with the bikers, but my dad wanted my mom and me to remain at arm's length from the shop. Daddy always compartmentalized his life.

In my early thirties, I sat on the Nova Scotia Advisory Council on the Status of Women. In one of our meetings, a colleague stated that all bikers mean to intimidate and are anti-women. I was shocked to hear her say it, and I quickly came to the defense of bikers. That exchange prompted me to write a column in the Halifax *Daily News* about the false way certain men are stereotyped in today's society.

My dad and brothers may have exhibited stereotypical masculine traits. They were big men who sometimes had tempers and carried their burdens quietly. They hunted for the meat that we ate all winter. They built our houses. They represented shoulder rides and whisker burns for me. They were gentle, and they made me feel safe. They laughed easy and they loved their families. Billy painted beautiful pictures and loved wearing pink shirts. Sidney, who was wild and free, cooks for his wife every day of their lives. The bouncer, Baby Guy, loves his kitty cats so much it makes him cry to even talk about them. So yes, they were bikers, they were tough guys and they were good men. They have been the best men in my life. In many ways, they are the only men who have never let me down.

My brothers founded a motorcycle club called the Roadriders. Often when I talk about the Roadriders, folks picture the Hells Angels. The Hells Angels are what is referred to as "one-percenters." That term stems from the fact that about one percent of motorcycle clubs are actually engaged in illegal activity as a business. When the TV series *Sons of Anarchy* came out, I found it so hard to watch because it seemed to me that they were trying to depict a one-percenter gang but giving the characters the qualities of non-one-percenters.

The Roadriders had their meetings in our basement, went on long-haul motorcycle runs to places like Old Orchard Beach, Maine, every year and also rode in the town parade most summers. They were a colourful cast of characters. When I look at some of the newer Harley drivers out there tricked out in all their fancy new gear, they look so shiny. The Roadriders wore leathers that were so old they were as soft as butter. Their colours—the jean vests worn over the leather displaying the club's insignia—were dirty. Most of them had long hair. A lot of them had beards or mutton chops.

And as a little girl, nothing, to me, was as exciting as when the Roadriders were going on a run. They would all gather in our front yard up on the compound. There would be maybe thirty Harleys idling out front. If you have ever heard one Harley, you know how loud they can be. Imagine thirty of them idling, and this was before noise by-laws required the tailpipes to have silencers on them. I would get on my knees on the couch by the window to watch them kicking them over. When I say, "kicking them over," I mean kick-starting. Back then, you had to kick-start a bike; there were no electric starts. My dad used to say if you're not strong enough to kick it over, you shouldn't be driving it. To kick-start, you bent out a peg on the side of the bike, and then with your body weight, you would kind of jump up, kick down on that peg and it would ignite the engine.

When I close my eyes, I can still see all the leather and long hair and hear the sound of all those bikes kicking over. The smell of the exhaust would waft up to me and I would run out the back door and stand on the rise just outside our dining room window, and I could feel the rumbling of those motorcycles in my chest. And it would excite me, and I couldn't even name it then, but now I know it was the birth of a sexual excitement that, still, when I hear a motorcycle crank open, stirs those same feelings in me. I would stand there listening to those bikes rumbling and then watch them get into formation, always with my brothers in the lead, and they'd go down over the hill and I'd stand and watch until I'd see the last dirty red bandana going over the train track. After they disappeared from sight, I could still hear them. There was this wonderful sound as they'd get down to the bottom of the hill and almost grow silent. I knew they were waiting to pull out onto the road. Then came the lower-range rumble of them pulling out, and still I would wait. Finally, the distant, higher-pitched sound of them filled the air as they all changed gears, rounded the bend in the road and opened up their engines. Roaring free down the highway to places as yet unknown to me. I would always stand there and listen as the sound disappeared on the wind.

There was a freedom and an excitement that those experiences represented to me. I knew that whatever direction my life went in, I wanted it to be exciting. I wanted to feel free as I knew those men did. I have always seen life as an open highway in front of me, and I am always excited to see what awaits me after I make the next turn and open my engines. I wasn't entirely sure how society looked at us back then, but we were not a conventional family and this was not a conventional business. And I like that. I liked it a lot.

We did have a couple of experiences with one-percenters as well. A couple of members of the 13th Tribe rolled into the compound one late-summer afternoon. They were a one-percenter motorcycle gang that eventually amalgamated with the Hells Angels. These particular three guys were on their way to Quebec City, and they were having trouble with their bikes. Someone had told them that there was this old Indian man and his son up on a mountain who could fix them up. They found their way to our place. Sidney took one look at the bikes and told our father that they were a mess. Daddy told him he didn't care if Sidney had to use fishing wire and chewing gum, he wanted those bikes fixed and fixed well enough to get them all the way to Quebec City. My father feared nothing and no one, but he did not want these dudes hanging around the compound any longer than they had to.

I have some sad memories of the business, too. There were so many people I knew growing up who ended up dying on their motorcycles. It was difficult having someone around the shop all the time and then seeing their bike being hauled into the yard after a fatal accident.

The death that really left the biggest impact on me was a young guy named Danny Hachey. I think it was because he was so young and sweet and because he was the first person I really knew who died. (I was so young when my grandmother died, I didn't really get it.) I knew Danny because we were in majorettes together and his parents owned a gas station in town. They had two children. Danny was their only son, and then they had a daughter who was closer to my age. Danny loved bikes and he used to hang out at the shop all the time. He was saving money for a bike, and Daddy gave him the opportunity to work around the shop to earn money. His parents were so opposed to him getting a bike. They were worried sick that he would get hurt on it. Danny said to them, "Look, if I die on a bike, I'll die happy." He just wanted a bike so badly.

Danny's parents finally gave in and Danny got his bike. A few short weeks later, one beautiful summer evening, he was driving down Victoria Street in Dalhousie and a car suddenly cut him off. He was thrown over the handlebars and into the front end of the car. He died on the scene. He was eighteen years old. Daddy got the call to go get the bike. He brought the bike back, put it in the back of the shop, and that is where it stayed for a long time. Daddy was really fond of Danny and that death hit him particularly hard. A few years ago, Danny's little sister, now a grown woman, sang at my mother's funeral. We chatted afterward and I told her how often I think of her brother.

For Daddy, his word meant everything. He assumed others were the same, and as a result, he got burned a couple of times in the business. My mother would get so frustrated with him. There was one time when someone we didn't know left his bike with us for repairs. My brother spent many hours repairing it and putting new parts in it. When the man came to pick the bike up, he asked to take it for a test drive before he paid for it. My father, being the trusting guy he was, said yes. My mother told him to make the guy leave his girlfriend at our place to ensure he would come back to pay. Daddy declined.

The girlfriend jumped on the bike and away they went. We never saw them again. It hurt him, like many things in life hurt my father, but it didn't shake his trust in other humans. He believed that your word was your bond, and although that didn't seem to translate to his marriage, it did translate in every other part of his life.

I bounced a cheque when I was seventeen, and when my father found out, he was livid. I think that was the angriest I had ever seen him. He could not believe that a child of his would put her signature on a piece of paper and not honour it.

From my perspective, our most interesting customer in all the years Daddy ran the shop was a woman named Paula. She was a professor getting pretty close to middle age. She had dark hair that was greying at the temple. She was the only female motorcycle owner that came to our shop. She would pull into the yard with her girlfriend on the back. Her girlfriend was tall and beautiful, and she was about twenty years younger than Paula. My brothers used to fawn all over her. About thirty minutes after they arrived, Paula's husband would pull into the yard in his car.

With the mainstreaming of polyamorous relationships, this might not seem avant-guard anymore. But in small-town New Brunswick in the mid-seventies, everything about that situation was groundbreaking. Paula was the first woman I ever saw driving a Harley. It didn't escape me that Daddy respected her because she knew her bike and knew how to handle it. She was the first "professional" of any gender I had ever seen ride a Harley. Paula and her girlfriend were the first same-sex couple I had ever been exposed to. And then there was the husband? I used to lie in bed at night and try to figure out how it worked . . . with the three of them.

I don't think I realized it at the time, but the motorcycle shop had a big impact on my life. It shaped my identity, empowered me to work for myself and even affected the physical traits that I find attractive in men. When my dad would complain about my taste in men, I often said to him, "You raised me in a biker dealership. Did you really think I would grow up and marry a banker?" That shop planted notions of anti-establishment and anti-conformity in my head. It also presented the notion of working for yourself. For the majority of my life, my father was his own boss. He quit a good job to take a chance on himself. For an illiterate, Indigenous, recovered alcoholic to take that kind of chance in the early seventies was bold. I followed him. I have lived by my wits for almost a decade now.

No matter where I am, whenever I hear the sound of a Harley, I think of home and I think of the scruffy, diverse cast of characters who rode in and out of my life over those years . . . each one of them leaving a bit of themselves with me, each one of them helping to form the young woman I was becoming.

SCENE 5

The one where I tell you about even-stevens

People often ask me where I get my self-confidence from. I never have to hesitate when I'm asked that question. I'm self-confident because I was given so much love and attention from my brothers and sisters, and yes, most especially from my parents. I always felt like I was the centre of their universe. I felt like every decision they made was based on my well-being. I always felt safe as a child. My wife is a child of divorce, and when she tells me stories of her childhood, I can't fathom the concept of being a child and not feeling absolutely and totally secure.

As I've told you, I grew up in a house of adults. And given that we were out of town, up on a mountain, I wasn't exposed to many kids. I spent most of my time in the house with my mother. I liked to colour, make arts and crafts, read and dress my dolls with the outfits my mom knit for them. When it came to physical activity, my parents and adult siblings were my playmates.

But to just go outside with a bunch of kids and play? Well, what's the point of that? In fact, on the first day of school, I asked if I could stay inside and colour during recess. To my horror, I was told I would in fact have to go out and play with the others. I walked out onto that playground and it looked to me like a scene from a zombie outbreak movie. All these wild-faced kids were running after one another. I turned on my heel and hightailed it right back into the school. "There is something wrong with them," I yelled. "They are chasing one another!" Poor Mrs. Lawlor spent that recess explaining the concept of tag to one very serious and skeptical kid. To be honest, I still don't get the appeal of the game.

I quickly figured out, however, that at school, boys and girls were treated differently. I observed that at school the boys were always the ones telling others what to do. And I observed that at home, my dad was dominant over my mother and that he raised his sons and daughters with completely different rules.

I can't put my finger on the exact moment that the word "feminism" or its concepts entered my conscious mind. But I can tell you that as far back as my memory stretches, I had a very clear idea of a concept I called "even-stevens." If someone got more pizza than me, I noticed. When Mommy was reading *Cinderella* to me and I heard how the stepsisters were treated as opposed to our heroine, I noticed. Later, when Jessica Savage took her seat at the anchor desk of the American news we watched on our only cable channel, I noticed.

I don't think that is unique to me. Most kids have a strong sense of fairness from an early age and can tell you if something is even-stevens or not. What made me different was that I was keenly aware when the imbalance I was experiencing was due to being a girl and I would never take it sitting down. I had a killer instinct when it came to even-stevens.

I didn't know it at the time, but looking back now, I realize it was my parents' relationship and their polar opposite personalities that turned my need for fairness into full-blooded feminism. My dad was a male chauvinist and my mother was, in my opinion, under his thumb.

Mommy and Daddy were born in the 1920s when the roles for men and women were very different. My mother was a study in contrasts. She was taller than most women of her generation and physically very strong, but incredibly timid and unassuming. She didn't swear or drink or raise her voice. She was emotionally very strong as well, quietly supporting the emotional well-being of each one of us, but she would rarely express her own feelings except for how they pertained to us—her love, pride and joy for us. I never heard her express her own wants and needs.

Every day, 365 days a year for the better part of seventy years, she put three meals on the table. She made her own bread and cookies and cakes. All summer she harvested the bounty of our land, and in the high heat of the summer, she stood at the kitchen stove putting up her preserves: jams, pickles, beets, chow all sat row upon row in their jars ready to be opened through the winter, when we would taste the summer freshness and all the love she put into each jar. She cleaned the house, put the sheets on the line every week so we could sleep with the heavenly smell of the east wind in our bed linens. She toiled in a quiet, dignified way and never wanted to be singled out or have attention brought to her.

Daddy was a different story. I think he was naturally a fairly sensitive person, but his childhood caused him to hide that sensitivity with a very sharp tongue. He was "old" my whole life. Comically, I am older now than he was when he had me, but what can I say, when you are little kid and your dad is fifty, he seems old. His body was twisted up with arthritis, which added to my assessment of him as old. Ironically, the same disease has now taken my youthful stride from me. Although I saw him as old and feeble, I would find out later that in fact he was known all his life as a man who could handle himself, which is to say he could physically defend himself and for most of his life was forced to do so. Even without formal education, he was incredibly smart and capable, and he had pulled himself out of a life of alcoholism that began in puberty and lived the final fifty-one years of his life in sobriety.

My dad was on the shorter side, I think about five feet, eight inches before age and arthritis shrunk him down closer to five foot six. He was shorter than my mother but there was no doubt who was dominant between them.

For the first seventeen years of my life, I was the apple of his eye, but the bane of his existence at the same time. I called him out on his language every chance I got. I remember the first time I heard him say, "So-and-so got herself pregnant." I was scared to even scratch myself never mind masturbate. I thought I could somehow get myself pregnant. Of course, I eventually realized this was just another way of my father putting all responsibility on the woman when something went wrong. After that, every time he used that expression, I would tell him lesbians everywhere wanted to know how so-and-so got herself pregnant!

The first big battle I remember—besides the ones that took place daily at home as I tried to change my father's thinking—actually happened at church. Our church was built the year I was born. It is a very modern design for a church. It is massive and made entirely of wood with a beautiful marble floor. The wooden ceiling is flat and incredibly high. There is no stained glass and even the stations of the cross are carved out of wood. I watched family members walk up that isle for weddings and funerals and baptisms. I was raised Catholic and that meant I studied my catechism all the time. But every Sunday, I would watch as boys served Mass. The cool outfits and the important spot that altar boys held looked super fun to me. I asked if I could serve Mass. It seemed like a reasonable request. Our priest at the time was ancient, and he quickly dismissed me by saying that girls NEVER serve mass. The logical question presented itself to me without even thinking about it: "Why do I need a penis to wash the priest's hands and ring the bells?" They called my parents.

After weeks of back and forth, I was finally able to serve Mass. I felt vindicated to take my own walk up that aisle as an altar girl. I washed Father's hands when the time came and folded the crisp linen napkin expertly when he was done with it. After Mass he told me I had done a good job and that he would see me next week. I declined. It had never been my intention to do it every week. I just wanted to make a point. Girls could do the job every bit as good as boys. Even-stevens.

Daddy didn't know what to make of my argument, but he was proud of me. Of course, a few years later, when I came to the full realization that a woman could never be Pope, a priest or even a deacon, I decided to leave the church due to the misogyny. Daddy was no longer proud of me and my arguments. He said if the Catholic religion is good enough for the Pope, it should be good enough for me. Well, of course, if you made me the head honcho of an organization that has its own bank and total autonomy AND you gave me a glass car to drive around in while you worshipped me, well then it would be good enough for me, too. But as long as I would be a second-class citizen, there was no way I could continue to go every week and put money in the collection plate. He made it clear that as long as I lived under his roof, I would be Catholic and I would go to church every Sunday. I went along until I was nineteen.

Years later, on the one-year anniversary of my brother Billy's death, my mom told me they would be saying Mass for Billy. I made the six-hour drive from Halifax to Dalhousie and joined the rest of my family for Billy's Mass. We filled a whole pew, and despite my rejection of the church, I was comforted by the familiarity of this.

On Sundays growing up, it was usually just my mom, Dad and me going to church. Sometimes also my sister-in-law Aloyse, but she usually went on Saturday night—she was and is a hardcore Catholic. She came from a family of nuns and nurses in New Waterford, Cape Breton, and if you ever found yourself in real trouble, getting Aloyse or any of the MacSweens to pray for you was a good idea.

For Christmas Mass back in the day, however, our whole clan went. I was always so proud to prance into church among these giants in my Christmas best. My dad would lead us in and then stand at the end of the pew as the whole family, almost two dozen of us, filed passed him. It gave me the same warm, "I belong" feeling I always got when we did anything together as a family, from hockey games to trips to Levesque Mill to swim in the summer. Being with my entire family continues to be one of my greatest joys in life.

Now, to find myself back at the St. John Bosco Church, sitting with my family, I wondered why I had ever turned my back on this tradition. Then the Mass began and I patiently waited for the priest to mention my brother. Fifteen minutes in, I leaned over to my mom and inquired about it. That's when she told me they don't actually say his name during Mass. The family pays a fee and his name is included in the back of the weekly bulletin—a bulletin not many people read and that gets thrown out from week to week. Oh right, that was one of the reasons I turned my back on this warm, fuzzy tradition.

Later in the Mass, the priest read from the gospel and then began his homily. "Women," he said, "obey your husbands." Oh, it was on like *Donkey Kong*! As he ventured further and further down the road of advising wives to compromise to keep peace in the house, this from a guy who was never married or even lived in sin, I got more and more angry.

When we arrived at the restaurant for brunch, it was obvious to my family that I was in a foul mood. Once we got seated and ordered (get the food taken care of first—that is the rule at all Palmater gatherings), one of my siblings asked me what was wrong. "That homily," I declared, barely able to keep my voice under control. I looked around the table seeking out faces who looked like they sympathized. Absolute blank looks in everyone's eyes.

It turns out I am the only one who actually listens to what is being said in church, which perhaps explains why I'm the only one who left the church formally. The rest of brunch was filled with me trying to figure out why they go if they aren't even listening. I mean, isn't the whole point of going to be lifted up? I was still too young, even at close to thirty, to realize that most of the things people do, not just in my family but in the world in general, are simply because they've always done them. So there I pictured my mother, sitting at Mass week after week, thinking about what she was going to cook for supper that night or what her next knitting project would be, perhaps even having some scandalous daydreams brought on by those Harlequin romance books she loved to read, thinking about any number of things, but definitely not listening to the guy doing all the talking. This gave me insight into how she stayed so peaceful in her marriage for so long. It also taught me to constantly question why I do things. So often, we continue with things that are not serving us just because. I wouldn't be where I am now had I not been challenging myself along the way. Take a look at your life and examine the motivation behind the things you do; it may surprise you.

Doing something because it is what is done also turned out to be the reason my mother used to sign her name Mrs. Guy Palmater. I didn't get around to questioning this practice until I was in grade six. Although I accepted that she took my dad's last name, I really couldn't understand why she used his first name as well. When my report card came home that year, I told her I wanted her to sign her own name to it, not Daddy's. In talking about it, she said it was just what women did "in her day." I did notice, however, that once I told her I didn't want her to do it on my report cards anymore, she stopped doing it everywhere else, too. In fact, as the years went by, she began taking small steps to get out from under my father's thumb: her own credit card, her own photo identification (no amount of prodding could change the fact that she didn't have, and never would have, a driver's licence).

I noticed, and so did Daddy, that she was getting more assertive. At mealtime in our house, Daddy and I would sit and Mommy would put the meal on the table. Once she was finished eating, she would head back into the kitchen to put the kettle on. A cup of King Cole tea was served after every meal in our house.

One Sunday, when some of the family was over, she waited a few minutes before putting the kettle on, and Daddy took the opportunity to point out that he thought she was "slipping." What he meant, of course, was that she was slipping in what he thought were her duties. To everyone's amazement, she raised her voice to him. His eyes and his temper both lit up, and he told her he would have to "straighten her out." This didn't refer to anything physical. It was simply him raising his voice and asserting his dominance in our pack. I remember this as though it happened only yesterday. She came to the kitchen door with a butcher knife in her hand and said, "You wouldn't have the balls."

Now understand this: My mother never, I mean never, swore. She also didn't say words like vagina or penis and certainly not balls! She went on to say, "Candy doesn't take your shit and I'm not going to take it anymore either!" That was a turning point, not only in my parents' relationship, but in my relationship with my dad. For years after that, he would tell me, "I had your mother trained for years until you came along." I was never able to get her to emancipate herself entirely, but I was proud as I watched her take more and more freedoms as time went by.

At first, I thought it was only my dad who did not think women were equal, and I honestly believed it was because he didn't have an education. In my young mind, any person with an education would realize how ridiculous it was to suggest that a girl was worth any less than a boy. I knew girls were different from boys, but not less than boys, because nothing in science class or history or social studies showed me any proof that I was less than. I figured people thinking women were inferior was the same as the poor, ignorant fools who used to believe the world was flat. They just didn't know any better. Now everyone knows the world is round. And now everyone knows that women and men are equal. I know, I know, how naive.

At school I was a bit like a bull in a fine china shop when it came to my assumption that everything would be even-stevens. If there was no girls basketball team (and some years, there wasn't), I just showed up at the boys' team tryouts. When the boys' hockey team got more accolades than the girls volleyball team for winning provincial championships, I took it all the way to Town Hall through a column I wrote in the town newspaper, the *Dalhousie News*. I challenged the mayor in my column and it played out like a small-town drama. That mayor is still a great friend and someone who comes to the compound for visits often. I had crushes on boys, but unlike so many of my girlfriends, I tried very hard to not let my crushes know. I never wanted anyone to have "one up on me." Also, in grade six, a boy said I was too ugly to date, and I wasn't over that yet.

My advocacy for women has continued throughout my life. What started as a simple, little-kid notion of even-stevens has turned into a life of pushing the boundaries of what girls and women can do and be.

My development as a feminist and as a self-confident girl would not have happened as quickly if it were not for sports. When I began playing competitive sports, I found something that made me feel powerful. I knew I had a natural talent, but I also knew I wasn't reaching my full potential as an athlete. My high school volleyball coach, Emery Johnson, showed me how to find that potential and how to reach it. What a gift to find someone skilled enough to take me to the next level, instill confidence in me and also be able to call me out on my shit.

Emery, more than anyone else, taught me about my own power and how to harness it. He also provided the yardstick by which I have measured every other teacher, mentor or boss that has come into my life since. Emery first made an appearance in my life when I was in elementary school. He was a phys ed teacher and a team coach at the local high school. He was training his class, which included my sister Sharron, how to teach athletics to younger kids, so he brought them over to my school. They had set up an obstacle course, divided my class into two teams and made it a relay race. When my turn came, I got to the part of the course where there was an exercise mat on the floor. "Do a somersault," they were yelling at me. It might as well have been a foreign language. I had never heard of a somersault and had no idea what it meant. My sister, realizing I didn't get it, said, "Just roll, Candy, do a roll." I dropped to the mat, lay stick straight with my arms by my side and rolled along the mat the way a pencil would roll along a desk.

At supper that night, I was heralded with stories of how embarrassed Sharron was when Emery asked her why her sister didn't know what a somersault was or how to execute one. I had no idea that night that this Emery person who my sister thought so much of would one day be a driving force in my life.

By the time I reached junior high, I had finally been socialized and found a school sport I loved. I was playing both volleyball and basketball, but basketball was my heart. I had posters of James Worthy, Nancy Lieberman and Kareem Abdul-Jabbar on my walls.

By grade nine, I was fairly tall but didn't yet feel powerful in my height. Deep inside me, I felt there was a great basketball player, but I wasn't living up to that potential, no matter how hard I worked on my skills. That year, Emery offered to have me work out with the high school volleyball team, although I wasn't old enough to actually play with them. He explained that by working out with them every day, I would become a much better player by the time I was eligible to play in grade ten.

The first thing that seemed so different about him was that he took my athletic dreams as seriously as I did. He knew that most of my mental energy was centred on basketball, and he very gently suggested I shift that energy over to volleyball. There wasn't really much of a female basketball program at my school or the neighbouring schools. He recognized that without a strong program and heavy competition, it would be very hard for me to develop in any meaningful way as a player. To sharpen your blade, you need hard stone to rub it against. He didn't belittle my dreams. Instead he helped me see how I would have a greater chance of achieving them: "So, you want to be a provincial champion basketball player? Well, that may not be possible given the realities, but you could be a provincial volleyball champion." Different sport. Same dream. What a lesson to carry me through life. I'm always running down a dream, but I keep my eyes open to alternative ways to achieve that dream. At the finish line, it doesn't always look the way you thought it was going to when you started.

It wasn't a likely coach–athlete match, Emery and me. He was francophone and white. I was anglophone and Mi'kmaq. He had a quick temper. I was very soft-hearted. Although at that age, it was hard for me to trust people outside my family, I grew to trust him very much. I always felt that he could see this special thing I had inside of me. He could tell that I knew it was there, and he never made me feel embarrassed by it. I never had to hide my light from him or make myself smaller. He taught me to protect that spark and gave me the tools I needed to make it erupt it into a flame.

In the years that followed, Emery pushed me harder than anyone else in my life had ever pushed me. And the harder he pushed, the better I became. It was the most glorious feeling to discover the full potential of my own body. At an age when most teenage girls are at war with their bodies, I was enraptured with mine because of all that it could do.

Just as I was revelling in being big and powerful, he taught me to respect those who were small and quick. He actually taught me that lesson on the badminton court. I was bragging about being tall, so he challenged me to a game of badminton. He ran me all over that court and beat me without breaking a sweat. He wasn't trying to humiliate me; he wanted to humble me and have me understand the strengths of other players. Embrace my power. Respect his speed.

As hard as he pushed, he was also very careful not to go beyond what I could handle. On a particularly stressful day, when homework, student council responsibilities and teenage hormones were piling up, I lost my cool at practice and shed a few tears in anger. That night, he called to check on me and let me know that if I needed to take a night off from practice from time to time, I should talk to him. Of course, I would never dream of missing a practice, but it meant the world to me that he cared enough to check on me.

I always felt that Emery had my best interests at heart. Knowing myself as I do now, I realize I am not an easy person to coach. I am strong-willed, I have a mind of my own and I push back against authority. He made me feel special. I realize now that he had this impact on many of us. I'm so fortunate to have come in contact with a coach who had the skill to bring out the best in me. Not every coach, teacher or boss has it.

As I said, I had dreamed of being a provincial champion. In grade eleven, I was the only non-senior on the starting volleyball lineup, and I found myself at centre court at Sussex Regional High School playing for the provincial championship. As the final point played back and forth at the net with my hands in the middle of it, I finally landed the winning point. It was like a scene out of a movie. Everything in that moment felt like slow motion—I saw the ball hit the floor on their side of the net and then I turned my head to see the umpire cross his arms over his chest, the symbol to indicate the game was done. Victory was ours. I turned toward the bench looking for Emery.

Time sped up again as he came running toward us, and I picked him right off his feet, surrounded by a cheering team. The connection that each of us felt with him and each other in that moment was unique. We had collectively set a goal, we all sacrificed and worked toward that goal, and now we had achieved it.

The year after we won the provincials, the entire first line, except me, graduated. It was a rebuilding year. My friend Monica and I were the two seniors left from the provincial team and we were playing with much younger players who were less experienced. Although we didn't do very well as a team, I spent a lot of that year strutting around like a peacock. I was better than these younger players and I liked showing that off when I could. I was team captain and I was feeling very confident that at the end of the year, I would also be the Most Valuable Player.

The team cast secret ballots to vote for MVP. I went to the sports banquet feeling completely confident that my name would be on that trophy. When Emery made the announcement, he said there was a tie. My friend Monica and I were both named MVP.

I tried my best to cover up my disappointment. Two days later, I dropped by the gym and Emery asked me into his office. He wanted to talk about the MVP award. He told me that the girls had indeed voted for me, but that he overrode the vote and added Monica because he did not feel that I had earned the prize.

It was such a blow to my ego. I felt betrayed by him. He then went on to explain that he'd wanted to see me lead this young team. He expected me to put the needs of those younger players ahead of my own needs. He talked to me about my performance in games, pointing out that when my game was off, I would crawl into myself, and the rest of the team could feel that from me. He told me that as a leader, I should have shaken that off and presented a confident face for those young players. That is what he expected of me and I had failed him in that. I would love to say that I got it instantly and walked away completely understanding his perspective. But I was seventeen and he was my coach, so yes, it stung for a bit.

But with time and perspective, that proved to be such a valuable lesson for me in life. I'm so grateful that he cared enough about me to explain his decision. And that he helped me to understand that my "natural" leadership abilities were not enough. He taught me what it truly meant to lead. I have used that lesson in every aspect of my life since. I have pushed myself to live up to his expectations of my leadership.

In all aspects of my life since high school, I have looked to find other great coaches. From the practice of law to my TV and radio career, I am constantly seeking mentors, bosses and directors who are exceptional coaches. I am also fiercely protective of myself and my gifts when I suspect that I am encountering someone who is not up to the challenge. A really skilled coach can push you beyond your own boundaries but should never shake your self-confidence. A great coach should demand excellence while at the same time convincing you that you ARE excellent.

My skill in sports gave me a lot of self-confidence, but my parents contributed to my body confidence, particularly my father. As a plus-size woman, I walk through the world unapologetically. When I was a child, I wasn't fat, but I was a big girl. I was almost eleven pounds and twenty-four inches long when I was born. I was always way taller than all the boys in class, with wider shoulders. My brother owned a bodybuilding gym. I used to work out at the gym. Gyms weren't plentiful then and you rarely saw women, never mind girls, in them. I was muscular and strong. I had long legs and no boobs! Until I gained weight in my thirties, I couldn't even fill a B cup. In fact, I gained one hundred pounds before I moved from a B cup to a C cup.

Growing up, I had two older sisters who had the largest natural boobs I had ever seen in my life, Sharron in particular. I have a hard time buying hats because my head is so big. I could take one of the cups from Sharron's bra, pull it over my head and there was still tons of room in it. There was more fabric in my sister's bras than there was in my jeans.

As a girl, I was thinking, "Okay, well, they must be on their way. I must be going to get my boob delivery any day now." All my friends started getting their boob deliveries, and I still had no boobs. My mom got me a little Daisy Fresh bra just because my nipples were starting to swell a bit, but I think the Daisy Fresh was just to make me feel better. When thirteen and fourteen rolled around, I still had a flat chest. I was a late bloomer in a lot of ways. I didn't get my first period until I was sixteen. The period I could wait for, the boobs I was getting impatient about!

By the time I hit sixteen, I still didn't have any boobs. I have a very large rib cage, and when I was on the beach in the summer, my ribs stuck out more than my boobs did! I even went to see a doctor to ask about having my rib cage broken and reset so that it might make the boobs look bigger. Finally, my mom said to me, "Sweetheart, you're going to have boobs like your mother, not like your sisters. Stop waiting. They're not coming. What you've got, that's what you've got. You're not getting any more."

For some reason, that really bothered me, to the point of obsession. It probably had something to do with the way teenage boys react when girls get boobs. I had crushes on boys, but I was afraid that when I actually wanted to date, my lack of boobs would negate my chance of success.

I would talk about it and talk about it. I remember asking my family doctor if it was possible to get a boob job in northern New Brunswick, and if so, how much it would cost.

Finally, my father had enough. After supper one night, he said, "I want to talk to you about this boob thing." Can you imagine? A sixteen-year-old girl talking about boobs to her senior citizen father! Good grief. What I expected was the usual parental drivel about how pretty I was to him or how it was the inside that counts. All that is true, but when you are in the throes of teenage angst and the world as you perceive it is wrapped up in whatever your issue is, those platitudes are not helpful.

This is what my father said: "First of all, let me just say, any guy that gets to know you is going to love you, but there are two types of men in this world. There are boob men and leg men. Sweetheart, there's no question: a boob man is never going to turn his head when you walk into a room. But I've got to tell you, you've got more legs than a bucket of chicken. They're long, they're in great shape because of all the sports you play. You're outside all summer, so they're tanned. You know, a leg man would crawl across broken glass to get to those legs. So instead of spending all your time worrying about what you don't have, why don't you just keep your eyes open for people who are into what you do have?"

Mind-blowing. I walked into my bedroom, stripped down to my French-cut cotton Jockeys and stood in front of my full-length mirror. I had thought about my legs often. I thought about how much weight I could push on the leg-press machine. I thought about how high I could jump. I thought about how powerful I could move on those legs. But that night, for the first time, I looked at my legs, really looked at them. And damn it, he was right. They were spectacular. I bought a bunch of short skirts that summer and never again worried about my tiny boobs.

For a man with no education who was barely parented himself, my father came through with what I thought was a brilliant piece of parenting. Be proud of what you've got. Some will love it, some won't. But don't worry about those who don't. It was a notion that I have applied to so many parts of my life. Even in my entertainment career, whether I'm onstage as a comic or on my television show or my radio show, I don't expect everybody to love what I've got, and I don't worry about the people who don't. There are people out there who do like it and that's just fine by me. Even this book: I hope you're loving it, but if you don't, that is cool with me. I'm happy to tell this story to the people who are picking up what I'm laying down. You have no idea how much stress that removes from life.

During that conversation, he also encouraged me to ask my three brothers what they were attracted to in women. He was driving home the idea that attraction is as varied as human beings are. This was particularly impactful to me because it was the eighties and popular culture had a very narrow vision of what was considered sexy or desirable in women.

I asked all three of my brothers to name a celebrity who best represented their dream woman. Baby Guy told me it was Farrah Fawcett. It was the answer I was expecting and was ready to go back and tell Daddy he was wrong.

Billy told me his dream woman was Mimi Rogers. She is a lesser-known actor who was briefly married to Tom Cruise. She was a brunette with a lazy eye. I was surprised. She was pretty but what about her eye? I asked him. He told me he found that little imperfection to be the sexiest thing about her. Then he said that Gloria Estefan was a close second for him.

When I asked Sidney, without hesitation, he said Barbra Streisand. That really shocked me. She certainly didn't fit the eighties' stereotype of pretty. For Sidney, she was the sexiest woman alive. That exercise opened my eyes to the idea that there's something for everybody. Not everyone likes the same thing. In the eighties, everyone wanted the same nose. Now everyone seems to want the same teeth. Everyone is trying to meet a false, often unattainable standard. I've learned that every single thing about you is uniquely yours; you just have to learn to dig it.

For me, my dream woman is Sophia Loren. Sophia Loren then, Sophia Loren now. She has the most beautiful face anchored by that strong Italian nose, which she thankfully never altered. I like being me, but in my younger years, if I could magically change my face, the only two faces I would have ever considered were Sophia Loren and Annie Lennox.

I interviewed Jeanne Beker a few years ago. I've always looked up to her as a broadcaster. I told her how I used to watch her on *The New Music* and thought she had the best job in the world. I told her how, in the eighties when beauty was so pedestrian, I found her beauty to be so sophisticated. She kind of cut me off and said, "Oh, yeah, with my big Italian nose." And I thought, Yeah, your nose just like Sophia Loren's nose, the most beautiful woman that ever lived. Because I think Jeanne Beker is drop-dead gorgeous, and had she ever changed her nose, I don't think she would be. Then she would have been just another face in the crowd.

Much of personal strength depends on accepting who you are, but also being *seen* for who you are and being given the freedom to be that person. Yet again, my parents came through for me in my formative years, but this time around music and what it did to me.

My taste in music has always been on the louder, harder side. My sisters didn't have a lot of influence on me musically, but my brothers did. I remember hearing Jethro Tull, Led Zeppelin, Deep Purple and Black Sabbath, and I loved that music. I started asking for that music fairly young. In fact, my mother bought me my first Black Sabbath album. When Meat Loaf's *Bat Out of Hell* came out, which seems tame by today's standards, a lot of parents were outraged. The album cover featured a picture of a half-naked guy on a motorcycle ripping out of a graveyard. (It was a picture that my brother Billy painted on a motorcycle a few years later.) The picture on the back of the album was a long-haired dude with his hand on the back end of a fast-looking woman. It didn't require the

Parents Music Resource Center putting a sticker on it to make it seem a bit much for most parents. Many of my friends were not permitted to own it. Their parents would not let them have it and would not let them listen to it. My mom went out and bought me the album.

From time to time, *The Fifth Estate* or *60 Minutes* or some other program on TV would warn parents about heavy metal music and how it led to devil worship. Many parents bought into the hype. But my parents, who were older than most, always let me listen to whatever I wanted.

Daddy was a big music lover and one day he said, "Come on, kid. We're going down to Roger Bernard's," which was the electronics shop in town. He bought this beautiful, big Pioneer stereo. It was an amazing eighties-type stereo with the record player on top, a double cassette deck so that you could make recordings, a tuner, an amp and two huge speakers. Classic. We also got this beautiful Kenwood for the car. Every Sunday was music day in our house. The TV remained off. After we got home from church, my dad would power up the stereo, and all day we would alternate: one of his records, one of my records. I assumed my mom's taste was in sync with Daddy's. When I grew up, I realized her taste in music was very different from Daddy's. She never asked to play anything different when I was a kid, and sadly it never dawned on Daddy or me to inquire.

It was wonderful to be a teen and not have my musical taste censored. One day I came home from school, in grade nine or ten, and my parents said, "Sit down. We want to talk to you about your music." Oh no, here we go. I was sure some news program had got the better of them.

They informed me that there was an album I was listening to daily and they did not like the effect it had on me. They said, "When you listen to it, your personality changes. We feel like it makes you sad, and maybe even a little depressed. And we're not taking the album from you, but we don't want you to listen to it as much. Maybe once a week, and maybe save that for the weekend."

As they were speaking, my mind was quickly shuffling through my record collection and trying to figure out what album it was. Kiss's *Destroyer*? *Sabbath Bloody Sabbath*? *Led Zeppelin II*? "The album we are talking about," they said, "is Chris de Burgh. *The Getaway*."

When I say Chris de Burgh, you are probably thinking "Lady in Red." But long before "Lady in Red," there were the *Crusader* and *Spanish Train and Other Stories* albums. These albums were filled with songs that told intricate stories, and I loved them. I was a huge Chris de Burgh fan. In 1982, he released *The Getaway* and I played that album multiple times a day every day. That was the album they wanted me to limit.

As they were explaining their concerns, I realized they were absolutely right. At the time, we were in the middle of the Cold War and there was unrest and strife in many parts of the world. I was just becoming politically aware. That album was all about oppression and reflected the times we were in. I was a very sensitive kid; hell, I'm a very sensitive adult. That album did make me feel anxious about the world I was growing up in. I agreed that I'd listen to it on the weekends only.

I had friends whose parents paid so little attention to their lives. Parents who were wrapped up in their own dramas and not paying particular attention to the fine-tuning of their children. I felt then, as I still do now, that I was blessed to have two adults paying such close attention to me that they recognized how particular albums affected my emotional well-being.

I've often thought about how much the adults in my young life influenced me and how they played such a big role in shaping the strong feminist woman I am today. I made sure that both of my parents knew the impact they had on me before they died. I can clearly attach them to so many parts of my life. Years after graduating from high school, when I found out my coach, Emery, was dying of cancer, I sat down with pen and paper and explained what his coaching meant to me. The letter was followed by a visit with him just weeks before he died. I was able to explain how I've used the things he taught me all throughout my wonderful life. He was among the adults who took me seriously and made me feel loved and important at an age when a lot of kids feel invisible. I am comfortable in my own skin. I know who I am. And I'm grateful to my parents and my coach for helping me get here.

Don't get the wrong idea. They didn't pass on the Caramilk secret to me, and then I magically became who I am now. I took their teaching, but then I turned and walked out into the world on my own. I embarked on many adventures, good and bad, to get here. My twenties were when I really figured out how resilient I was. Because my twenties, well, they weren't for the faint of heart . . .

SCENE 6

The one where I begin to make A LOT of mistakes

One of the themes I really want to get across in this book is the acceptance of mistakes and the idea that mistakes are the juiciest parts of life. I have always learned more from my mistakes than I have from my wins. It is in the hard times that our character is built. I had no idea, rolling into my twenties, how many mistakes I would make, how low I would fall or how important the experiences would all be in the long game of my life.

High school was so fun. Don't hate me. I know a lot of people hated it, but I truly loved it. Every aspect of it—sports, student politics, teachers, friends—it was all so much fun for me. When it came to an end at the age of seventeen, I was excited about my future, but I was also very melancholy about leaving high school. I worried that life might never be quite as sweet as it was at that moment. I was right about that and I was wrong about that. Meaning, it did get worse, then better, then worse, then better. Now I realize those are the cycles of life. I now know that by experiencing some of those lower moments, the higher moments have been made even sweeter.

I fell in love with the city of Halifax, Nova Scotia, when I was about fifteen. My best friend at the time was quite a bit older than me, and she was in the pharmacy program at Dalhousie University. I took the train up to visit her on my March Break in grade ten. For a small-town girl like me, this city seemed perfect. With seven major post-secondary institutions, it was teeming with young people. And with more bars per capita than any other city in the country, there was a booming nightlife. On our summer trips to Montreal, I was a bit intimidated by the big city. Halifax, however, was like a big town. It was big enough to have good concerts but small enough to feel familiar. Even though I was young, I was almost the height I am now and was able to sneak into many of the bars with my friend. I knew I wanted to live in Halifax, so my plan after graduation was to go to Dalhousie University.

Alas, like all good plans, it got derailed. Dalhousie did not accept me. Halifax would have to wait. I enrolled at St. Thomas University in Fredericton, which was only three and a half hours from home and was a Catholic school. Both of those facts thrilled my parents. The summer between grade twelve and first year of university was an exciting one, and I thought I would escape it without incident. I was wrong.

My best friend and I used to love going to Ben's Tavern, a pub in Campbellton. We went just about every Friday and Saturday night . . . my folks didn't know! Two weeks before heading to university, I got dressed up for a night at Ben's. I was wearing a white silk blouse buttoned to the neck with a pearl brooch covering the top button. It was tucked into a skin-tight, houndstooth pencil skirt that ended mid-calf and had a slit in the back. I was also wearing four-inch black pumps. I kissed my folks good night and Karen picked me up at about eight thirty (young people went out much earlier then). When I got to the bar, for some reason I started drinking my draft too fast. Suddenly I was hammered. I'd thrown up in the popcorn bowl by ten. I've often wondered about Karen's next decision.

I usually came home around 2:00 a.m. So Karen could have put me in the car and let me sleep it off for three or four hours. Instead, she put me in the car and drove me home. She stood me at my back door, knocked on it and drove away. My mother opened the door and there I was. The brooch was gone and the top two buttons were missing off my blouse. There was puke down my right sleeve. The pencil skirt was twisted sideways and the slit was torn to midway up my thigh. There was a brief moment when Mommy and I just stared at one another, neither of us speaking. Then she asked if I was drunk. I nodded my head.

She brought me through the living room, where my father was watching the nightly news. I remember him staring at me in stunned silence, one of the few times I ever remember my father being speechless. Mommy undressed me, put me in bed and told me we would talk in the morning. The moment my eyes opened on Saturday morning, I was petrified. I didn't want to get up because I didn't want to face them. I had never done anything even close to this before, and I couldn't imagine the kind of trouble I was going to be in. Little did I know that what was coming was way worse than punishment.

My mother and father walked into my bedroom crying. They sat on either side of me. My father put my head against his chest and started rocking us back and forth, murmuring, "Where did I go wrong? This has to be my fault." It was pure torture. I pleaded with them to stop crying. I was trying to convince them that all my friends' parents had already gone through this. In desperation, I said, "You guys didn't make any mistakes. I am still a virgin and almost none of my friends are!" I begged them to just punish me. Take my car keys from me. Ban me from using the stereo for a week. My father said he couldn't punish me for something that was his fault. Alcoholism, he was sure, had just claimed his baby.

I remember my sister-in-law asking me why I couldn't have just held off the partying for two weeks, until after I was away at school. I tell you, my dear old mom and dad never saw me drunk again. Never ever! I made sure of that. But the party had started and it didn't really stop for the next five years or so. And the guilt that I felt over those tears didn't slow me down.

While I couldn't wait to leave home, I am also a sentimental person, so when it came to packing for school, I wanted to bring EVERYTHING with me. All my framed pictures, all my posters, all my books. I couldn't imagine leaving any of it behind. I filled the suitcases that Sidney and Ginette had given me for graduation and then I proceeded to fill a trunk that Sharron had given me. I had seen so many American movies set in universities, and in those movies, the dorm rooms were huge. Well, it turns out that items on the TV may appear bigger than they are.

We pulled out of Point La Nim in our AMC Eagle station wagon. It was a cooler kind of station wagon because it was four-wheel drive and kind of resembled the small SUVs on the road today. All that aside, however, it WAS a station wagon. Mommy and Daddy were in the front seat and I was in the back along with some boxes. The suitcases were in the hatchback. And that steamer trunk? You guessed it, strapped to the roof . . . just like in the movie *Revenge of the Nerds*.

We arrived on campus at STU, and my dad yelled at two young fellows to help him get the trunk off the roof, because my father was, by then, an older man, and he was on crutches due to a knee replacement. At the time, I was mortified that my dad was commanding these two cute boys to help him. But if I'm being truthful, I am the same way now that I use a cane myself. I will ask strange young men on the sidewalk to give me their arm when it is slippery.

Between me and the cute boys, we got the trunk off the car and the boys carried it up to my dorm room. When I opened the door and saw where I would be living for the next nine months, I realized I had overpacked, seriously overpacked. The room, which I would be sharing with a roommate, was set up the way I imagine a prison cell is set up. Bed, desk and closet on one side; bed, desk and closet on the other side, with about three feet of space in between the two sides. We emptied the trunk so they could take it back home with them, but I told them to leave the rest to me and insisted that they go. My mom was okay, but I could tell it was hard for Daddy to leave me.

I finally convinced them to leave and I began setting up my room. Thirty minutes after my parents left, there was a knock on my door. I opened the door to find my father standing there on those crutches with big tears in his eyes, saying, "Are you sure? Are you sure you want to stay?" I assured him that I would be fine and rushed him back out to the car. I was so excited to start my independent life, to be a "grown-up." Little did I know, it would be more than a decade before I actually grew up.

That year in Fredericton was a blur of great friends, drinking, dancing and partying. A drinking and dancing establishment called The Arms received the bulk of my student loan that year. I had some fun, but it was, in essence, my lost year. It was the first and probably the only year in my life during which I was not moving toward something. There was no goal. At the end of it, I felt so empty. It seemed like my friends knew where they were going, and I didn't. I knew I wanted to set the world on fire. I knew I wanted to have an extraordinarily big life, but at eighteen, I had suddenly stalled on my climb to great things. At the end of it, I told my parents I didn't want to go back to Fredericton and that I wanted to take a year off to figure out my next move.

I stayed home in northern New Brunswick for a year. I got it into my head that I would be a physiotherapist. I thought this might be a way for me to continue to be involved in athletics. I had never shown interest in science courses at school and the thought of putting my hands on strangers' bodies kind of grossed me out, but I didn't let that discourage my new plan. I worked part-time at the drugstore in town and also attended science classes part-time at the high school.

While attending those classes, I became close to a boy I had known all my life but had never hung out with. I will call him Christopher. As the school year progressed, Christopher and I realized how much we had in common. We were both incredibly sarcastic and would often try to "out quip" one another.

In the summer following that year, after a lifetime of saying "No snotty-nosed boy from this jerked-off little town is going to take my virginity," I lost my virginity to Christopher. Having sex was like discovering kryptonite. I couldn't figure out why everyone wasn't having sex all the time. This was even more fun than playing sports! Suddenly, I understood the attraction of being a "bad girl."

In September of that year, I entered a science program at the University of New Brunswick. I knew as soon as I arrived back in Fredericton that I had made a mistake. I didn't like living in Fredericton the first time, and I liked it even less the second time. I spent that whole year begging my parents to let me drop out. They insisted that I had to stay. They thought I was floundering, but I think they felt helpless about how to help me. They thought that insisting I stay in school would in some way keep me on track. They were mistaken.

Christopher had gone to Dalhousie University (the school I wanted to go to) and was living in Halifax (the city I wanted to live in). I, on the other hand, was living in Fredericton in the basement apartment of some crazy woman's house. The basement apartment had a serious earwig problem, and she had strict rules that I could not have anyone spend the night or even visit me during the day. I had to walk through a path in the woods to get to campus, where I spent most of my time. Being the gregarious extrovert that I am, this living arrangement wasn't ideal. A few months later, she evicted me for having an overnight guest. I didn't tell my parents.

I ran into a friend from home, Lynn LaBillois (who would years later become Chief of Eel River Bar First Nation). She had a tiny little hatchback car. She helped me move my things. In what felt like a million trips, we transported box after box of my possessions from that basement apartment to various dorm rooms all over STU and UNB campuses. Every friend who had a bit of space was storing a box for me in their room. I had no idea what to do about my furniture, but the landlady solved that problem for me. She put my furniture in the snowbank outside her house. I was, for the only time in my life, homeless.

Meanwhile, my parents had not heard from me in some time and were getting very nervous. There was no way for them to call me; I was supposed to call them. They started calling the university, and finally the registrar's office told them they should call the library, that perhaps they could post something for them. Otherwise, they didn't know how to help them get in touch with me. For two weeks that winter, there was a large banner at the entrance of the main library, a long sheet of the old, perforated computer paper scratched in with heavy black marker that read "Candy Palmater, call your father."

Meanwhile I was sleeping on the floor of friends' dorm rooms and lounge couches around campus, and sometimes I would just stay awake all night killing time until the sun came up. At night, I would sneak into dorms so I could shower. I buzz-cut my hair, very close to my head so it would be easier to care for in my homeless state. I just had to make it to the end of Christmas exams, then I could call my parents to come get me for the Christmas holiday without telling them anything that was happening.

After calling the library, however, my parents called the landlady, at which point, she told them that I could "peddle my wares somewhere else." She informed them that she evicted me and that my furniture was in the snow in her front yard. My parents called my cousin Phil, who lived in Fredericton. He came to get my furniture with his half-ton truck and asked me why I hadn't called them when I got evicted. That, he informed me, is what family is for. He didn't understand that I was trying to hide all this.

During this month of chaos, all I wanted was to get out of Fredericton and see Christopher, so I started hitchhiking . . . a lot. The first trip was with a friend of Christopher's and it was planned. But after that was successful and as soon as I had a few drinks, I would get bored of where I was and want to be in Halifax. Often, I would tell my friends I was going to the bathroom, but instead I would leave the bar we were in and head to the nearest highway and start hitchhiking. My friends tried taking my coat check ticket, thinking that if I didn't have my coat, I wouldn't leave.

On a very cold winter's night, we were at the campus bar in Fredericton and I got in some kind of a dust-up with another woman. I can't even remember the details of how it happened. I just know that there were some broken bottles involved, and my hands were bleeding at the end of it, and I just decided I wanted to go to Halifax to see Christopher.

So I walked out to the highway by myself, with no coat, in the winter. Up until then, I had been so lucky. Every time I hitchhiked, it was always transport truck drivers who picked me up, and every time, they were family men who would lecture me about hitchhiking by myself. Often, they would radio other trustworthy drivers to hand me over to, in order to get me to Halifax safely. I've always felt, even as a child, that the universe was looking out for me, that the universe or God, or that energy force, had a plan for me and that it would keep me safe so that I could execute that plan. This is a comforting feeling, but I realize now, it also gave me a false sense of safety.

There I was on the highway alone, in a black turtleneck and winter white pants covered in blood, hitchhiking. A transport slowed to a stop about twenty-five feet past me. It was so cold that sound was muffled by the snow. I can still hear the air coming out of the brakes and the sound of the truck idling as I turned toward it. The sky was dark and the red lights on the back of the truck were glowing like lights on a Christmas tree. The passenger door swung open. I started running toward the truck. For the first time, however, I had an eerie feeling. That little voice we all have inside us that keeps us safe was telling me not to get into that truck, but I couldn't hear it clearly through the Jack Daniel's fog in my head. I kept running toward that truck.

When I got to the open passenger door and looked up, I realized there were two men in the truck, the driver and a passenger. The man in the passenger seat had a bottle of booze between his legs. Drunk as I was, without hesitation, I pulled myself up into the truck and crawled over the passenger into the sleeping cab. The passenger passed the bottle to the driver. He had a drink and offered it to me. I declined. I asked what he was pulling and he told me it was a shipment of packaged foods. It was late, I had been drinking for hours, all I wanted was to sleep.

As I stretched out on the bunk, I decided that if I felt the truck slowing to a stop, I would wake up and get myself to safety before they could try anything. It didn't dawn on me that I was trapped with two men in a truck travelling at a hundred kilometres per hour. I have no idea how I thought I would get myself to safety, but that was my plan as I passed out.

Sure enough, I felt the truck start to slow down not long after. I sat up quickly in a panic but was instantly relieved to see we were stopping for gas, not pulling off on an abandoned road. I only had a few moments to experience relief before the driver, in his drunken haze, hit the gas tanks. He didn't knock them off the platform, but he did hit them. It felt like RCMP, fire and ambulance appeared instantly. They took the driver and passenger out of the truck and stuck their heads in to see an eighteen-year-old girl sitting in the sleeper section with bloody hands and jeans. The officer asked if the two men had done that to me. I reassured him they hadn't. They asked me for my ID, which, thank goodness, I had. I handed over my UNB student card. They came back with my ID and said, "The driver has blown the breathalyzer way out of the water. He's going to be arrested. We'll get back to you and let you know what's happening."

I lay back and closed my eyes again. I remember that the vibration of the idling truck allowed me to fall back to sleep. When I woke up, everybody was gone. The ambulance was gone, the fire trucks were gone, the police were gone, the driver and the passenger were gone. I was sitting in this idling transport. I remember looking at it, thinking, "Could I drive this thing?" And if you've ever been in the cab of a transport, it's not at all like a regular car. I quickly realized attempting to drive the truck was a bad idea.

I grabbed my shoulder bag, climbed down out of the truck and headed into the twenty-four-hour diner attached to the gas station. The waitress and all the patrons were staring at me. I realized they were looking at the dried blood on my jeans and the cuts on my hands. The waitress asked me if she could get me anything, and I said, "No, I don't have any money. But if I could use your pay phone?"

There was a little table right underneath the pay phone. I sat at that little table. She brought me a cup of tea, even though I couldn't pay for it, and a warm wet cloth to clean the blood off my hands. The buzz had worn off and I was suddenly scared. I called Christopher in a panic, and I said, "I was in a truck, I was trying to hitchhike to you. I'm in some place called Jemseg, New Brunswick." Which, as it turns out, is not that far outside of Fredericton at all. Without hitchhiking, I didn't know how I could continue on to Halifax or turn back to Fredericton. I was stuck.

Christopher, being the pragmatic guy he was, said, "Look in your bag and tell me what you've got." I opened my purse. I had a bottle of beer, a can of Static Guard, an extra pair of underwear and thirty-five cents. This is what I brought with me to hitchhike to Halifax. We agreed that that wasn't going to get me anywhere. He suggested I call the highway patrol. At the time, there was a New Brunswick highway patrol in addition to RCMP. So, I called the highway patrol. I explained my situation. They said, "How old are you?" I said, "Eighteen." And they said, "You're getting back the same way you got out there." And they hung up on me. The highway patrol was clearly not going to be the answer to my problem.

In my continuing panic, I called a friend in Fredericton. My friend Andrew, who, incidentally, went on to become an RCMP officer, used to drive a cab part-time. I thought maybe he could come and get me if he was driving that night. He was dead asleep. I was waking everybody up on campus. Everybody was in a panic along with me. They called the RCMP. The RCMP told them the same thing the highway patrol had told me: "She's eighteen years old. If she's missing for two days, call us. Other than that, she's on her own." It's true, I was on my own.

I asked the waitress if I could stay in the diner until daybreak because I was too scared to hitchhike in the dark. She took pity on me and I spent the night sobering up in the diner, wondering how my life had come to this. At the same time, however, I have to admit, I was high on the excitement of it all. I had been so protected, so sheltered, so goal-oriented up until that point. There was something about the wild nature of what had happened to me that night that I loved. I knew I didn't want to throw my life away, but I knew sitting in that diner that I wanted to have more experiences like this. I didn't want to be reckless, but I would be lying if I said I wasn't titillated about how wild that night had been.

At daybreak, I thanked the waitress and walked back out to the highway to find a drive back to Fredericton. An old man in a pickup truck stopped for me. He offered to bring me to the hospital to have my hands looked at. I declined and mumbled a clumsy lie by way of explanation. He pretended to believe me. I told him I was trying to get back to Fredericton; he told me he was on his way to Mass, just ten kilometres down the road. I said that at least I would be ten kilometres closer. Then I laid my head against the passenger door window and fell asleep.

And a few moments later, he gently woke me and said, "Where is it that you live in Fredericton? I'll skip church this morning and I'll take you right there. I just can't in good conscience put you out on the side of the road." I told him where I was going, and he pulled into a little country convenience store and bought a bag of Mrs. Dunster's donuts. They're made and sold only in Atlantic Canada. I had never had them before that Sunday morning when I shared a bag with a kind of man from Jemseg. He let me eat half the bag—it was the first time I had eaten in two days. He drove me into Fredericton and handed me what was left of the donuts. To this day, the taste of a Mrs. Dunster's donut makes me think of my crazy night in Jemseg and the kind old man who brought me back to safety.

My friends in Fredericton were furious with me. They didn't speak to me for days, and even when they resumed, something had changed between us. My wild antics had gone from being entertaining to being over the edge. Shortly after, I went home for the Christmas holidays. I secured a place in residence and returned to school in January. But I had already decided on that Sunday morning that I was done with school.

There was a deep yearning in me to break free. The disapproval of my friends and family were not enough to deter me. I had decided I was going to push the boundaries of my life and see what existed out there on the sharp edges.

It was 1989. I, and the rest of the world, was immersed in Mötley Crüe, metal music and the wild over-the-top lifestyle being represented by that scene. It was all about wild boys with electric toys, tattoos, big hair and Jack Daniel's. I loved the music and I wanted to live the life. I decided I was done with school and I was done with being the golden child of the family.

While I might have been a wild thing away from home, I wasn't ready to completely disappoint my parents. I couldn't just tell them I was dropping out of school to pursue sex, drugs and rock 'n' roll. So instead I told them a giant whopper. I told them I was going to join the military and I was going to Halifax while I waited for the call to basic training. In actuality, I wanted to be close to Christopher and I wanted to be where the action was. In Atlantic Canada, in 1989, the action was in Halifax.

Over that summer, I made plans with my friends Sheila and Anne Marie. We would move to Halifax together in the fall. I couldn't wait. Right before the move, Christopher and I had a horrible fight in which I threw a full can of beer at him and he told me he never wanted to speak to me again . . . and he didn't for almost two years. I moved anyway. I had a plan. I would live in Halifax for a year or two, then move to Toronto for a year, and then head down to Los Angeles. I had no real plan for what I wanted to do in LA, nor had I contemplated moving to permanent summer when my favourite season was winter. But in my mind then, Sunset Strip in LA was the wildest place on earth at the time and I wanted in on the debauchery.

In September of '89, I moved to Halifax without a job. I had money from my summer job and I applied for Unemployment Insurance, the dole. Billy and Aloyse drove me and my stuff to Halifax in my father's truck. They had met there in 1967 and they loved the city. My father and I argued over me taking a double bed with me. Once my mother convinced him I could just as easily have sex in a single bed, he relented. Daddy had been so emotional when they dropped me off at university, but on the day I left for Halifax, it was my mother who became emotional. She stood in the front yard and cried. I didn't understand why she was sad. She explained that university was temporary. I still came home in the summer. But now, I was moving away for good. She looked at me and said, "I'm in my sixties and all I have ever done, my whole life, is look after my babies. What do I do now?" Heavy. In the years that followed, I unpacked that statement and understood it more deeply. In the moment, however, all I could do was tell her I loved her, I would always be her baby, but I had to go. This time, I cried, too. I was twenty years old.

It was a beautiful sunny Halifax day when we pulled up to the apartment building on Quinpool Road where Anne Marie and Sheila had found us a two-bedroom apartment (one of us would sleep in the living room). I looked down Quinpool Road with such excitement. Almost like I was looking down the road of my life at all the possibilities that lay before me. Somewhere down that road was a dream. On that beautiful day, in the city I loved (and still love), all things seemed possible. I had no idea that a storm was on its way and things were going to get a whole lot harder before they got easier.

SCENE 7

The one where I meet an even bigger mistake at Tim Hortons

For the first few months of my new, independent life, I partied. I partied with my roommates and without them. As I mentioned, Halifax has more bars per capita than any other city in Canada. In my first six months there, I think I frequented just about every one of them.

On our first Saturday in Halifax, we took part in a longstanding Saturday tradition. Saturdays at Peddler's Pub was a rite of passage for anyone living in the port city in the late eighties and early nineties. The pub would open early and a local band called the Swell Guys would start playing shortly after high noon. They were a party band in every sense of the word. Their most popular singalong song was something called "Bestiality's Best, Boys." I'm sure you can imagine some of the colourful lyrics in that number!

By 3:00 p.m. every Saturday, the place was packed and everyone was three sheets to the wind. Peddler's was the first bar I was ever kicked out of. It was the first bar where I danced on a table and it was the bar where I ate mussels for the first time.

I was still pining for Christopher and hoping to run into him around town. But there was also a part of me that had begun looking for something more exciting. It was the dawn of glam metal and there were a lot of guys fronting as "bad boys." I was looking for the real thing.

In one of our arguments, Christopher had told me I was "not the kind of woman you marry." Maybe he was right. He was on his way to law school and was looking for someone far more conservative than me to settle down with. I was on my way to the wild side and looking for someone far more danger-ous than Christopher to NOT settle down with. I found him, about a year after I moved to Halifax.

After six months of partying, I knew the government insur-ance I'd been living off wouldn't last forever, so I started look-ing for work. I got a job at The Body Shop in the Bayers Lake Shopping Centre. I loved The Body Shop. I loved the products and all it stood for, so when they called, I jumped on it.

I learned everything about the products in the shop, about

the founder, Anita Roddick, and about how to sell. I loved working there.

One of my co-workers and I became really great friends. I was performing well in terms of sales and was feeling quite content. Then Mötley Crüe announced a show in Toronto at the SkyDome (now known as the Rogers Centre) as part of the Dr. Feelgood tour. I had to go. I called my friend Kelly, who lived in Toronto, and asked if she would go with me. I then called my mom to ask if I could buy two tickets on her credit card. Those two things secured, I had to figure out how to come up with the money to buy a plane ticket to Toronto. I looked in the newspaper, which was what we did back then to find a job, an apartment or what movies were playing at the theatre. I saw that Tim Hortons right across from my apartment was hiring for the back shift. I applied and got the job. I would be working from eleven at night until seven in the morning, which would give me just enough time to shower and get over to The Body Shop for 9:00 a.m. The pay was $4.35 per hour, minimum wage. When added to the five dollars an hour I was getting paid at The Body Shop, I thought I could save enough for my airfare.

Back then, Tim Hortons was just donuts and coffee. There were very few drive-thrus. People would park, come in, get their coffee, either stay or go. If they stayed, they smoked. The air was blue-grey from your knees up at all times. The Tim Hortons across from me was small but incredibly busy. It was non-stop twenty-four hours a day. And it seemed to me that it was the perfect solution. After working at The Body Shop in the daytime, I could come back to my apartment, sleep for a couple hours, get up, get into my Tim Hortons uniform and head across the street to work.

The very first night I worked at Timmies, that elusive creature I had been looking for, a "real bad boy," walked through the door. It would take me years to figure out he was actually just a garden-variety bad boy, but that night, to twenty-year-old me, he seemed to be something special. I clocked him instantly—he was six foot four and about two hundred pounds. Long and lean, he had a full beard and hair down to his belt. He was in a black leather jacket, jeans and black boots. He walked up to the counter, and the first thing he said to me was, "You've got a pretty mouth." It sounded like that line from *Deliverance*. But when he said it, I rolled my eyes, because I have full lips, and particularly in my twenties, I got a lot of suggestive comments from men about my lips. And when I rolled my eyes, he quickly said, "No, I mean you have beautiful teeth."

So began some very exciting and very difficult years of my life. It is hard to tell this story without looking at it through the lens of a fifty-two-year-old woman. I was someone completely different then, and although I thought I was worldly, I realize now I had been coddled by my family. He was thirty-six, I was twenty, and I imagine he saw me coming from a mile away. George became an intoxicating and dark chapter of my life.

The other women who worked at the store, the cab drivers who came into the coffee shop, they all told me to stay away from him. The more they warned me off, the more interested I became.

He had a lot of cars, and every time I saw him, there was a different woman getting out of those cars. I asked him direct questions and asked around about him, but I could never get clear answers. I kept chatting with him during my shifts at Tim Hortons and I kept saving money for the Mötley Crüe concert.

I had been working day and night for close to three months. I was sleeping every three days or so and really burning the candle at both ends. Two weeks before the concert, I got off work at seven o'clock on a Sunday morning. It was a beautiful, sunny Sunday summer day in Halifax. It was so quiet. The city was still asleep and I felt as though I had the streets all to myself. I was planning to go home and crash for seven hours or so, since I didn't have to work again until 11:00 p.m. that night. George was sitting in the parking lot waiting for me. He asked me if I wanted to go for a drive to Point Pleasant Park to smoke a joint. Of course, I said yes. I was so sleepy I could barely see straight, but it was nice spending time with him. We walked for hours along the water, talking about music and cars. All we did was talk. He dropped me off at my apartment at noon, and I fell into a deep sleep thinking about my morning.

We spent time together often over the weeks that followed. It was completely platonic, and I fooled myself into thinking he was a really sweet guy taking his time with me. Little did I know, he was just letting the fishing line out so as not to snap it. He was an experienced fisher. One night, before I started work at eleven, he walked me to the edge of my building, and we kissed for the first time. It was the kiss that woke me and it was the kiss of death all at the same time, and deep down inside me, I knew both were true.

Our love affair burned so hot at the beginning. I didn't want to worry about what he did for a living, even though nobody could tell me. Every time I asked what he did, people would just kind of roll their eyes. I would ask him, "Where do you work?" He would make jokes. I kept asking him how old he was, and he kept giving me different numbers, so I was never sure, and in fact, I'm not even 100 percent sure right now. A few years ago, before moving to Toronto, I found his birth certificate among some pictures of us from back then. The date on the certificate was, in fact, different from what I had thought it was for years. But given who this guy was, I can't be sure the birth certificate is valid either.

I didn't even know if he'd even been in jail. Turns out he had spent more than a decade in there. I didn't know he had kids. I didn't know he had a girlfriend. I should have known better. At my current age, he would never even get a first kiss from me. But I was so naive then and so in love. All my internal warning bells were ringing but I turned a deaf ear.

He was incredible in bed. Having sex with him was so different than any teenage sex I'd had until that point. I couldn't get enough of him.

So here I was, my parents' pride and joy, the shining hope of the family, former president of my school student council,

Little Miss Achievement, getting involved with the wrong man and loving every minute of it. We were driving in his car along the Bicentennial Highway one hot summer afternoon and the song "Candy's Going Bad" by Golden Earring came on the radio. We looked at one another and grinned. I reached forward, turned up the radio, then turned my head toward my open window. The sun was warm on my young, beautiful face, the wind whipped my long hair back over my shoulders and I felt so alive. In spite of all that followed, that memory still makes me smile.

My relationship with George was volatile. There were times that when we would fight—which we did often—the fight would get physical. I went through a window once because I was banging on his door. I knew he had a woman in there, and he wasn't answering. I kicked the window in to come through it, and he put me back out through the same window. We had fights where we laid our hands on each other, me screaming and kicking, even throwing things. This happened at home and sometimes in public.

When I think about these things now, they embarrass me, but at the time, I had a hunger for this wild experience. So as hard as it was on me, and as much as I was crying myself to sleep every night, I was addicted to the drama. I loved the excitement of it. I would look at my friends with their milquetoast boyfriends, having mediocre sex (as they complained about often), and I would think, "How do you even know you're alive?" There has always been something about me that yearns for something different. That still exists inside me, but I fulfill that hunger in more productive ways these days.

And I was falling deeply, deeply in love with him. I knew this was not going to be a "happily ever after." But I did think if I loved him hard enough, I could change him. This, I think, is the disconnect between men and women. Men marry women hoping they will stay the same forever. Women marry men hoping they will change in time. Neither get what they are hoping for.

I went to the Mötley Crüe concert but I didn't move to Toronto that year as planned. Because of George, I decided to stay in Halifax for a little bit longer. "A little bit longer" would turn into thirty years, many of which I spent with George. Those early years are a blur of either being at work or being in bed with him. I didn't sleep normal hours, I didn't work normal hours and I was no longer socializing normally. I was slowly losing touch with my friends, who were graduating from university, getting married and settling down. None of them (except my friend Nat) invited me to their weddings.

Talking about those exciting and difficult years is particularly challenging now because it was a time in my life when I was physically so capable and strong. I walked almost twenty kilometres every day to get to my various jobs. All my jobs involved me standing for eight hours. I was strong, young and beautiful. Physically, I could do anything. Given my current mobility issues, it makes me a bit sad that I wasted these vital years with a man who didn't treat me the way I felt I deserved to be treated.

At the time, though, I was so excited to be in the middle of it. John Mellencamp once sang about holding on to youth because life continues long after the thrill of living it. I was hell-bound and determined to hold on to that as long as I could.

At fifty-two, I am happy to report that the thrill of living has not yet gone! I'm still out on that edge. I'm just doing it in a different way. I learned how to take healthy risks that propel me forward instead of holding me back.

I've been in a stable relationship for twenty years, but it's with a woman, not a man. At forty, I walked away from a good job with the government and decided to go out on my own. I'm on the edge all the time, because I eat what I kill. If I don't work, I don't earn. It's all down to me. I still live the excitement of that edge, but it's not as potentially damaging as it was in my twenties.

When I think about my twenties, it's hard for me to marry the concept of who that girl was with the woman I am now. I couldn't begin to tell you the number of landlords that I screwed over because I didn't pay my rent. I was giving all my money to George. My parents were in constant stress worrying about me.

When I was twenty-five, I had some professional photos taken of me to get framed for my parents as a Christmas present. I'm in profile but staring into the camera with just the hint of a smile on my face. I got home late Christmas night because George was supposed to come with me, but we fought and he backed out at the last minute. When I arrived, my brother Billy came over to see me. My father was unwrapping that picture. He got very emotional and said, "Sweetheart, you are so beautiful." Billy was looking over his shoulder at the picture. The two of them were silent for a moment, looking at this picture of me. And then Billy said, with this look of disgust on his face, "Can you believe she's throwing that away on this loser?" Billy has been dead for twenty years and I've been separated from George for twenty years, but I remember that moment so vividly. For a moment, I could see how they saw me during that stretch of time. It makes me sad that Billy didn't live to see me get away from him.

During that time, I was trying to figure out how to put a life together. My motivation, quite honestly, was him. I wanted to get back on track so that I could look after him, so that I could give him a cushy life, so that he'd never have to work. Not that he ever seemed to work. But at the time, that's what I wanted to do.

So, I started talking to my parents about what my options were. I couldn't go back to university because I had an outstanding student loan that I wasn't making payments on. I could get work—I never had a hard time getting work—but it was all minimum wage. My parents suggested I get some sort of training that would allow me to find better-paying jobs. I was interested in taking a legal secretary course, but the tuition was fairly high and I had no way of getting my hands on that kind of money. A few weeks later, my parents called me and said, "We're going to give you the money for the legal secretary course." I think it was around $6,000, which was huge money, and I knew my parents were on a fixed income. I asked how they got the money, and they told me that Daddy's hunting camp had burned down and he was giving me the insurance money from it. Years later, I asked my mom about the amazing coincidence of the camp burning down just when I needed tuition money. She said, "I don't know anything about it . . . except that your father, crippled up as he was, left here in the middle of the night on a snowmobile with a gas can. The next day, we heard that the camp burned down. That's all I know. Go to school. Make your move and don't waste it." I made my move.

I took the legal secretary course, I learned how to type (a skill that has come in handy while writing this book) and I started looking for work with local law firms. I wasn't having much luck. Finally, I contacted the Native Council of Nova Scotia. A guy named Bill Pictou, who has since passed away, was the employment counsellor there. He told me that Dalhousie University had a personnel officer named Gaye Wishart who was actively trying to diversify Dalhousie's workforce. I called her, and she had me in for what she called an information interview. It wasn't about a specific job; it was just for her to meet me and talk to me about the opportunities that may be available to me.

That was the most fateful meeting of my entire life. The impact it had on me, both professionally and personally, was immeasurable. Gaye became my boss and my closest friend. She has had a front-row seat in my life for the past thirty years, but it all started with that first meeting.

We instantly connected. She recommended me for an administrative assistant job at Dalhousie's Henson College. I got the job. For the first time, I was earning somewhat decent money. I was still getting evicted on a regular basis, because I was still giving George so much of my money, but it was the beginning of my climb. I was finally back on the road meant for me. As the kids say, I was out in those streets and I was grinding! Years later, Daddy asked me if the secretary course was a waste of money. I assured him it wasn't: it paid for my ticket to ride, it put me on the road to this dream.

I worked for a year at Henson College, but then started working for Gaye as her part-time receptionist. That turned into full-time and then I started learning more and more within the office. I had talked about going to law school over the years, and when I was twenty-six, Gaye started really encouraging me to apply.

Gaye, her husband, Brant, and their two daughters, Jess and Ali, became my second family. I thought of their house as my home away from home. I spent most of my holiday meals with them and their extended family. Often, I would break my parents' hearts by not going home for Christmas or Easter to spend it with George. When he wouldn't show up, I would end up going to Gaye and Brant's.

I had filled out my application to Dalhousie law school but

had not submitted it. There was a fee of seventy-five dollars that had to be submitted with it. I didn't have it. Gaye kept bugging me to submit it and I kept putting it off. I didn't want to tell her I didn't have the money. I was so embarrassed about where my money was going. One day she said, "I'm going to the registrar's office. Give me your application and I will drop it off." I gave it thinking they would bill me for the money. The bill never came. I found out almost twenty years later that Gaye and Brant paid the application fee for me.

Dalhousie law school accepted me. After three years of working with Gaye and the rest of the folks at my office who had become my dearest friends, I was leaving this full-time job with a pension (unheard of in my little town) to go to law school. I loved the people I was working with so much. When Gaye went away on vacation, I used to complain about how dull work was. We had holiday dress-up parties and happy hours downtown, and we were also doing really important work. I cried openly on my last day of work because I knew I would never again have a work environment that good. And I was right.

To this day, my friendship with Gaye remains one of the deepest and most important friendships of my life. Brant died of cancer a few years back, which felt like losing a brother. I watched their girls grow up and cried at all their major milestones. I did Jess's hair and makeup for every major school function, and last summer I flew home to officiate Ali's wedding. They are like the kids I never had. I also developed deep bonds with Gaye and Brant's extended families and feel so connected to them. I have been blessed to have such a close family of my own and then to move away and become part of another really close family. I'm aware that many people don't experience family like that even once, and I've been lucky enough to have it happen twice.

SCENE 8

The one where Billy is dying and I can't get home

Being accepted to law school made me feel like I'd achieved the impossible. My parents were so excited that I think the excitement must have been twofold: they assumed the law school acceptance marked the end of my wild and crazy days and also it was just such a big thing for my family. Only one of my siblings had even graduated from high school. Now their baby was going to law school. Naively, I thought the hardest part was behind me. I hadn't actually thought about how I was going to support myself financially, do the classes and the work and balance the demands of my life with George.

George dropped me off for my first day of school. The Weldon Law Building is a beautiful glass-fronted building with steel and brass sculptures on the front step. Its modern architecture sits in contrast to the historical brick buildings that surround it. That day, the sun was shining and upper-year students were scattered on the front steps. Most of them were younger than me, and just about all of them seemed far more conservative than me.

Having quit my job, I had to start thinking about how I was going to pay my rent. I had a lease on a small apartment in a drug-addled part of Halifax. The building was owned by a woman who worked in financial services at the university. I was falling behind on rent again and fighting with her husband constantly about the situation. I knew I couldn't carry on that way, but I didn't have a solution.

I had been granted funding through the Indigenous, Black and Mi'kmaq Initiative. Years before, a man from a prominent Mi'kmaq family named Donald Marshall Jr. was wrongfully convicted and imprisoned for the murder of Sandy Seale, a young Black man. Upon Marshall's release after thirteen years of incarceration, the province of Nova Scotia conducted an inquest. It was determined that the lack of Black and Indigenous people working in the justice system was responsible, in part, for what happened to Donald Marshall Jr. As a result, the law school established this funding program that would waive the tuition for qualifying students as well as provide $500 a month to cover expenses. Despite this relief from the financial

burden of paying tuition, my personal situation was still tenu-
ous. In fact, the five years of my life that began with law school
and ended when I left the practice of law were the most stressful and turbulent years I've ever experienced. As wild and crazy
as my late teens and early twenties had been, I was young and
I had no responsibilities. At twenty-seven, it was time to get
serious about my life and where it was going to go. Law school
was a lot of work. I had financial problems all the way through
it and the drama with George did not calm down. It was in that
time that I realized my family was not invincible. The night
before I started law school, my mother had a massive stroke,
and in the middle of my second year, my brother Billy died. It
was also during those five years that I stopped looking after my
health, the impacts of which I am still dealing with today.

In spite of all that, I really did enjoy law school. I have
often thought that had I done it with less turmoil in my life, I
would have enjoyed it even more and I would have gotten even
more out of it. I already had a tight group of friends, so I didn't
socialize with people from school. In fact, I finished law school
without ever having set foot in the law school social club. I also
couldn't afford to go out.

In first year, I had Professor Innis Christie for contract law.
He had a very imposing presence. As the former dean of the
law school and a former minister of labour in Nova Scotia,
he literally wrote the book on labour law used in law schools
across Canada. Many students were scared of him. I loved him
instantly. We hit it off and he became an important part of my

law school experience. In second year, when my brother died, I was taking his advanced labour course. He called me at home in New Brunswick and told me to stay with my family and that we would sort things out when I got back to Halifax in the new year. When I did get back, he made arrangements to teach me the course one-on-one every Wednesday night. He would finish his workday, go home for supper and then come back to the school to teach me. It has been the greatest gift of my life that people seem to come along and help carry me across the rough waters every time I need them. After graduation, I kept in contact with him via email every few months. Sadly, about five years after I graduated, I came into my office one morning and found an email from his son informing me that Professor Christie had died of cancer. I told my secretary to cancel my morning meetings, closed my office door and had a proper cry. He was not in my life for a long time, but he left an indelible mark on it.

Somehow, through fights and makeups with George, battles with my landlord over my unpaid rent and mountains of school work, I made it through my first year of law school. My final exam that year was a torts exam. After I finished, I came home to my apartment on Evans Avenue and my phone was ringing. It was my mother. I will never forget her exact words: "Your brother has a little bit of cancer." I couldn't process it at first. For some reason, it never dawned on me that anything like this could happen in my family. Billy was the oldest, the leader of our family and like a second father to me. She told me he had esophagus cancer, but they would operate on him and he would be fine. I wanted so badly to believe.

I worked for Gaye that summer but still couldn't get caught up with my rent. The fights with the landlord were escalating and I knew I had to find a solution. That $500 a month I was living on through the school year made it hard to find an apartment. Luckily, I heard of a subsidized housing program called Tawaak Housing. They provided urban housing for Indigenous people and only charged 25 percent of my income for rent. I secured an apartment on Robie Street in Halifax. The rent would be eighty-five a month and yet there would be many times over the next two years when I would not be able to pay that.

On the day I moved into the apartment, I was so sad. I had never lived in such poor conditions. The apartment was the front, main-floor section of an old Victorian house that had not had any maintenance done on it. The ceilings were beautifully high and that was the only thing beautiful about it. There were bay windows looking out onto the street from the front room, where I squeezed my dining table in. At the very end of a long hallway was a tiny kitchen with a fridge, stove, sink and two cupboards. To the left was a small bedroom, and then there was the most disgusting bathroom I had ever seen.

My heart broke when I saw the bathtub. I love the ritual of late-night baths by candlelight, but this tub was only about three and a half feet long and it was permanently rust stained. Picture the sink in an old-time gas station bathroom in the seediest horror movie you have ever seen. That is what my tub looked like. I scrubbed it with every possible concoction and could not change the look of it.

For the first week in the new apartment, I bought sandwiches from the twenty-four-hour gas station across the street because I couldn't bring myself to cook or eat anything out of that kitchen. George, having spent ten years in prison, wisely told me time would make it better. People, he said, can get used to any conditions if they are forced to stay in them long enough.

The streetlights and the gas station just outside my bedroom window lit my room up all night long. There was a crosswalk with sounds for the blind. It was a busy street, so that beeping went on night and day. There was a loose manhole cover in the street that clanked every time cars drove over it. The man who lived in the apartment behind me partied five nights of the week.

But George was right. I eventually resigned myself to the idea that this would be my home for the next two years. I can't say there was ever a moment when I loved that place, but it was a roof over my head while I took on my final two years of law school. I couldn't afford a phone so I was relieved to find that there was a pay phone across the street. I got a pager for thirty-five dollars a month and tried desperately to not let anyone know I didn't have a phone. I was embarrassed. I did let Gaye know. I told Gaye almost everything . . . well, I told her more than I told anyone else in my life, except George. For

Christmas that year, one of my gifts from Gaye was a roll of quarters for the pay phone. I love that woman.

When second year started, my heart wasn't really into it. Billy had the operation to remove his esophagus during the summer, but he wasn't getting better. Mommy, who was in denial, kept saying he wasn't going to die. This man who was full of muscles my whole life was shrinking before us. I didn't want to be at school; I wanted to be home with him and my family.

I know I've told you about Billy, but I can't stress enough the monumental role he played in my life. He was the leader of our pack, and he treated me more like a daughter than a sister. When I was eighteen and seeing Christopher, Billy was clear that he really didn't like him. They played baseball together and Billy thought he was too mouthy. I always suspected the reason Billy and Daddy didn't like Christopher was because he was the first boy I was ever serious about.

One night around Christmas that year, I had borrowed Billy's car to go out with Christopher. We were making our way home at 2:00 a.m. in a huge snowstorm, and I made the decision that I would stay at Christopher's house. I figured I could use the snowstorm as an excuse.

I called Billy from Christopher's and said I couldn't get the car out of Christopher's driveway so I was going to stay over. I was supposed to work at the drugstore the next morning and I told Billy I would go straight to work from Christopher's house.

Billy wasn't stupid. He knew the family's driveway was on an incline, so regardless of the snow, the car would have rolled down the driveway as soon as it was taken out of park. Christopher's mother was home, but she kept a fairly loose rein on him, and besides, she liked me a lot. So Christopher and I spent the night in the basement, and we slept past the start of my shift. We were in his living room with his mother when I saw Billy's Bronco pull into the driveway. Without knocking, Billy stormed into the house. I was getting ready to leave anyway, so I had my green Far West winter jacket on, which was all the rage in the eighties. Remember, I was eighteen years old, technically an adult. I am five feet, ten inches tall, and at that time, I weighed about 165 pounds. Billy picked me up by the back of that jacket. The house was a split-level, and my feet didn't touch the stairs all the way back down to the front door. Christopher was sitting in a chair in the corner and didn't move. His mother didn't say a word. Years later, when I asked Christopher why he didn't defend me, he said, "Are you kidding? I was in the corner fear-peeing."

Billy was furious. He was yelling, "Kid, you are not going to spend the night at a boy's house. That is not happening!" He was shouting so fiercely, I could feel spit hitting my face. That was my brother Billy. He was so protective of me. And he was so proud of all of my accomplishments. He always made me feel beautiful, made me feel so accomplished, and he always watched my back.

Right before I got into law school, Billy needed open-heart surgery. He had been having chest pain, and the doctors weren't taking it seriously because he was in such fantastic physical condition. They finally sent him to Moncton to have his heart checked, and from there, they sent him directly to Saint John, New Brunswick, for heart surgery. He had a triple bypass and recovered wonderfully. We all thought that would be the end of his struggles.

I went home to see him after his esophagus surgery, just before second year started. When I pulled into the yard, he was washing his truck, but he was sitting on a chair because he didn't have the stamina to do it standing up. And although he was still larger than most men, he was way smaller than my brother Billy had ever been. I knew when I hugged him and felt the bones in his back that this was not a man who was getting better. On my second night home, he came into the house after supper with a helmet in his hand, and he said, "Get your boots on, kid. I'm taking you for a spin on the hog." We climbed on his bike in the front yard and my mom took a picture of us.

It was a beautiful late-summer night. As I slipped my arms around his waist, a waist I knew so well, he felt like a stranger. His body had changed that much. We drove through town, down through the reserve, past the beach and onto the country roads behind Charlo. The sun was setting as we traced over the territory that formed us both. We didn't talk much. We didn't have to. I knew he was creating one last memory for me. As the sky turned from red to purple, he turned us toward home. Just before we turned off the road to start the climb up the hill to the compound, he spoke to me over the roar of the motor. "Kid, this is your last ride with me." It was. And I have never been on a motorcycle since.

The first month and a half of second year went by with me in a haze. I kept calling home to see how he was, and my mother kept telling me he was going to be fine. Just before Thanksgiving, I called Billy directly and he told me he was dying. We had a long talk and he said something that changed the way I have lived my life. He told me he was angry that he was dying, but that he had lived his life exactly the way he wanted to. He'd driven his Harley all over North America; he'd skied on some of the best mountains. When he and Aloyse were young, they both quit their jobs, despite the protests of people around them, and they jumped on the Harley and drove across the country. He had a long and love-filled marriage and he had two beautiful kids. "So," he said to me, "I am angry that it is over at fifty, but I have done everything I wanted. I am not leaving anything undone." I was twenty-seven when we had that conversation, and I decided then that I needed to live my life the same way. I would leave nothing undone. I would say yes way more than no. When my time came, I would have the same peace he had facing his end.

I decided to go home for Thanksgiving that year so I could see him in person. That was the worst visit home I have ever made.

My sister Sharron was home and we were fighting terribly. It was hard to be in the same room together. She and my mother told me I couldn't go over to Billy's too much because it tired him out, which was so frustrating because seeing him was the whole reason I was home. I went over to see him the first night I arrived and I couldn't believe how he looked. The cancer was eating him alive. He lit up when he saw me and wanted to hear all about law school. I had just had lunch with Constance Glube, who was then Chief Justice of Nova Scotia, and he wanted me to describe the lunch to him in detail. When I left his house that night, I felt as low as I had ever remembered feeling. I cried from his doorstep all the way to our house.

When I was a baby, my parents made their will. In the will, they left our house and all the land to me, since I was the baby and so much younger than the rest. They wanted to make sure I was taken care of in case they died before I was grown. They made a provision for Billy and Aloyse to take care of me if they died when I was still a minor. As I came in the back door that night, crying uncontrollably, I remember Sharron and I getting into a fight about something. Then my mother chose that moment to tell me that she and Daddy had changed the will. Even though I was in law school, they felt that my life was too unsteady for them to leave everything to me. They worried, I think, that George would somehow screw up everything they had worked their whole lives for. So, they were leaving the land to all the kids equally and they were leaving the house to my sister Sharron.

That is one of the few times I ever remember being angry at my mother. I told her she had just ensured I would never have a home to come to once they were gone because I couldn't get along with Sharron and her husband. Here I was about to lose my brother and now my mother was telling me that I had just lost my home, too. I was the only child who was born and raised on that land. I have always wanted to be buried on that land. It always did and still does mean so much to me. I couldn't believe my parents were taking that from me. I felt like my life was falling apart.

On the Sunday morning, I was heading back to school. It was a bitterly cold October day. Billy came out onto his front step in his old blue robe, and I hugged him harder than I should have, considering how frail he was. I can still remember how he smelled as I had my face pressed against his neck. I can feel the scratch of his beard against my cheek and my tears rolling over our skin where we were pressed together. I disappeared into the comfort and familiarity of his arms. I said that I didn't want to go. He told me I had to go. He took me by the arms and pulled me away from his neck. He told me he loved me and to study hard. Those were the last words he ever said to me. There wasn't enough time. I didn't tell him all the things I wanted to tell him. I never saw him alive again.

I got back to school and tried to concentrate, but I couldn't stop thinking about the fact that I was missing his last days. Every time I called, my mother told me I didn't need to come home, that he was still doing okay. I told her over and over again that she didn't need to protect me from this. I knew he was dying, and I needed to be there when it happened. His daughter Vicky was home and kept asking when I was coming. They kept telling her it was too soon to call me. On a Wednesday, Billy and Aloyse came out of their house and waved to my parents, who could see them through the dining room window of our house. They were headed to the hospital. He never returned.

Finally, my niece Vicky told the family they had to call me or she was going to. Mommy paged me. I was at home studying. I pulled on a coat and ran out to the pay phone. "You better come home, baby." That was all she said. The cold wind was lashing at my face as I asked her if he was dying. Once again, she repeated, "You better come home."

I paged George to come over ASAP. I needed to get home and my car was not working. I had no money to fix it. But he did not drive me the six-hour trip. He refused. The fastest way I could get home was to wait until the next morning and take the train. George still refused to take me home. Billy died that night. This was the beginning of the end for George and me.

That night, still in Halifax, I had a dream about Billy. I could see his face, and he said, "Watch over the kids for me." And then the dream ended and I woke up. I looked at the clock. It was three thirty in the morning. I knew, in that place deep inside me where I know things, that my brother was dead. I lay awake waiting for a page that didn't come. I got on the Via Rail Ocean for the long, lonely train ride. For the nine hours I was on that train, I felt suspended in time. I knew this train ride was the neutral zone between Before and After.

The train stopped in Charlo. I manoeuvred my suitcase down the steps and looked up to see Mommy and Sharron standing there. I said, "He died last night." Sharron nodded yes and my mother embraced me. So much changed after that train ride. For me and for my family.

The whole family was gathered at Billy's place when we arrived. All my siblings and all their kids. I looked around at everyone and knew that none of us would ever be the same now that Billy was gone.

Looking back on that now, I realize just how right I was. Not only did his passing affect my family, but it touched so many other people, too. Many of the people he used to ride with sold their bikes because it was Billy who would organize all the runs. To this day, I get messages on social media from people he touched through his coaching and mentorship in baseball, skiing and his beloved Bill's Gym.

At his funeral, all the bikers put their Harleys back together (it was November so they had them put away for winter) and they formed this beautiful honour guard for him. They rode behind the hearse from the funeral home to the church. The church was packed. I, of course, was still in the car with the family, but one of my friends was in the church. She told me it was very quiet inside that packed church. Then the silence was broken with the sound of the Harleys approaching. In a stage whisper heard by all, someone said, "Billy's here now." I gave his eulogy, and at the end of it, I recited the A.E. Housman poem "To an Athlete Dying Young."

It felt like the whole family was adrift for a bit after he died. It took all the fight out of my father. It was the only time in my life when I saw my mother really brought to her knees. She told me often that the only reason she could go on was the five children she had left. He is talked about anytime we get together, and as I said, twenty-two years later, I still get messages from people whose lives he touched. I wish he could have seen that I did finally leave George and that my life unfolded in even more wonderful ways than he might have imagined. But there was still quite a bit of turbulence ahead before all that glory. Starting with finishing law school.

SCENE 9

The one where I learn a whole lot of lessons and not just in law school

I stayed home with the family until the winter semester started in January. Then I reluctantly headed back to Halifax. A strange feeling came over me as I took that trip for the thousandth time. As the scenery passed by, I couldn't understand how people just went on living their lives. How could the world keep spinning as though nothing had happened after the loss I experienced? I wanted to stop and scream. I had missed all my mid-year exams, which I would have to reschedule and prepare for. I also had a whole bunch of new courses starting, and all I wanted to do was climb into bed and cry. And on top of it all, I was broke.

Up until that point in my life, I'd always had multiple jobs. But law school was hard for me, and I couldn't have a job and keep up with my school work. So I knew there was no relief in sight. It all felt so overwhelming. When Billy first got sick, I was looking for a way to self-medicate. I knew I couldn't drink or use hard drugs to get myself through this because I couldn't juggle law school with a narcotics or alcohol habit. Food, however, was a "safe" way to get a dopamine rush and I could do it cheap.

That summer, I had started going to the grocery store around the corner from my house and buying the cheapest chips I could find. Usually, it was the store-brand chips at 89¢ for a family-size bag. I would take them home, and when I was alone, I would gorge on them. During the summer, when I was working and I had a bit more money, I would often order a big party pizza and hide it in the oven of my apartment, and throughout the night I would eat the whole thing. Many nights I went to bed with so much stomach pain I was sure something would burst and I would die in my sleep. But it numbed me. It dulled all the emotional pain. And I could eat and study at the same time. I was trying to hide it from George because I knew he was fat phobic. He had made derogatory comments about my sisters, who were always heavy, so I didn't want him to know I was binge eating.

It really didn't dawn on me that all this eating combined with the fact that I was now sitting on my butt all day long would result in weight gain. I have always been into clothes.

Even in high school, I would wear tight pencil skirts and three-inch heels to school every day. I wore suits a lot when I worked at Dalhousie University. When law school started, I began wearing gym pants and sweatshirts all the time. I'd always had a full-length mirror in my room since I was about nine years old, so every night when I got ready for bed, I'd get a good look at my body. I remember how I used to love to stand naked in the mirror and flex my muscles. In this crappy little apartment, I had one small mirror over the bathroom sink and that was it.

In February of second year, we had to do a moot court (a mock trial). So I had to dress up for the first time in a long time. I pulled out my favourite taupe suit. It was the suit I had worn when I had my interview to get into law school. It had pleated pants and a long, fitted blazer. It was still in the dry-cleaning bag from the last time I wore it over a year ago. George was lying in bed as I pulled the pants off the hanger and tried to put them on. I couldn't get the pants past my knees. They wouldn't go up any further. I looked up at him, furious, and said, "The dry cleaners gave me back the wrong pants and it was over a year ago. I won't be able to get my money back and this is an expensive suit." He had the strangest look on his face. He asked me if I was kidding. I couldn't understand what he thought I was kidding about. I was dead serious.

"You've gained a lot of weight, baby." My temper got hot. How dare he.

"I may have gained ten or fifteen pounds, but not enough to make these pants this small for me," I said.

"No, you have gained at least fifty pounds," he replied.

The next day, I went to my doctor and I got on her scale. I had gained eighty-five pounds and it had taken me less than eight months to do it. My doctor wanted to have my thyroid tested. She couldn't understand how I could have gained so much so fast. I told her to call Greco Pizza, they would explain it.

I don't know how this happened without me really noticing it, but it did. And it was like a runaway train. I had no idea how to stop it. It was one more brick added to the already heavy load I was carrying.

Thanks to the help of Professor Christie and my friend Monica, both of whom spent a lot of one-on-one time with me, I managed to get all my first-term exams done and somehow make it through second year.

During my early twenties, I started to learn more and more about Mi'kmaq culture and also about how racism works, both systemically and personally. At home, things for me were subtle. When I moved to a new city, things got more overt. People didn't know who I was, so they were truly just judging what they saw. Because of my mixed race, sometimes people were confused, but more often than not, people would just ask me, "Are you Indian?" At the same time, I was reading and learning more about our history. I had met an anti-racist activist named Anne Bishop, who taught me so much about how to navigate in racist systems. But I was still young and naive in many ways.

While I was dealing with so much personal turmoil, I was very active in politics at school, and at the end of that year, I was elected President of what was then known as the Aboriginal Law Students' Association. There were some power struggles happening at the law school between one minority professor and much of the rest of the faculty. It just happened that I had a personal beef with the minority professor, who I will call Professor Shields. Because I was so active in the politics of the school, I was vocal about my complaints around Professor Shields.

I found myself getting drawn into the power struggle that was happening with the faculty. It felt to me like many of the powerful faculty members were befriending me. And I liked how that felt. I enjoyed the attention and I thought they were looking out for me. It wasn't until years later that I realized some of those faculty members were using me as a battering ram against Professor Shields. In retrospect, it was so inappropriate for those professors to draw me into their drama, but draw me in they did. Years later, I took Professor Shields to lunch and apologized for the part I played in that whole scenario. She graciously accepted my apology. I had my issues with her while I was a student and I still feel those issues were valid, but I acknowledged that I had allowed myself to be used as a tool against her in a fight that had nothing to do with me.

I was so frustrated because it wasn't the first time this had happened. In my first job with Dalhousie University, I had been used by senior management against a director they were having trouble with. It made me feel stupid to have fallen into the same trap twice. Anne Bishop really helped me to understand that the pattern was a common one and happened to many Indigenous and racialized people who manage to rise up in institutions.

It was a valuable learning experience, though. I recall being in the car with a very powerful person from the law school who said to me—a student at the time—"I've gone through [Professor Shields's] financial statements to see if I could find anything untoward there because then we could easily get rid of her, but her accounts are all in order." Even then, that sent a chill down my spine. I realized, "Oh, that's how they come after us people of colour when they want to get rid of us."

So law school didn't just teach me how to use the law library, it taught me how racism works, in sophisticated ways. I was no longer dealing with some halfwit in the schoolyard calling me a spear chucker. I realized I was in deep water with very big and dangerous sharks. It was an education I put to good use, because the higher I climbed on my ladder, the more subtle and way more insidious the racism got.

The law was no longer an abstract concept of things done wrong in the past. I was reading the legislation and policy that dictated our lives as Indigenous people—in fact, our very identities. And at the same time, I was eyewitness to the subtleties of how it works with really smart people. It is so much easier to deal with some redneck who is bald-faced about his beliefs. When you are dealing with highly educated people who believe themselves to be liberal thinkers, it's almost like boxing with a ghost. It can drive you mad. You start to second-guess yourself. My time with the law, both in school and at the firm, was the time in my life when racism was most pointed for me. Before that, it was subtle but it didn't affect my course in life. Also, unknown by me, my brothers were sheltering me from so much of it. Afterward, I became wise to recognizing it and knowing how to protect myself from it. But during those years, it really wreaked havoc on my life.

Second year came to an end and I needed a job. I applied for some summer internships but did not get any. One of the managers from my former job at Dalhousie mentioned that his wife was looking for an administrative assistant to reorganize her office. I needed the work and had the skill set so I took the job. I had to use my first paycheque to buy some office clothes since none of mine fit. To my horror, when I got to the mall, I couldn't find clothes to fit me in any of the stores I usually shopped in. I made my first trip to a plus-size clothing store and was mortified to find that most of the plus-size tops had pictures of kittens or flowers on them. I could write a whole separate book about the perils of living life as a plus-size woman.

The woman I was working for, whose husband and son I adored, was unlike anyone I had ever had a relationship with before. She was from privilege and was not what we'd call woke today with regard to race and class, but she thought she was. It made for a bit of a difficult summer, but she meant well and she gave me a job I was so grateful for.

At the end of the summer, I learned another great life lesson. On the way to work one morning, I heard on the radio that Van Morrison was coming to Halifax. I loved Van Morrison, but I knew I would never be able to afford a ticket. I mentioned it to my boss (I will call her Cali). Turns out Cali loved Van Morrison too. Much to my delight, my end-of-the-summer gift from Cali was tickets to Van Morrison. The catch was that I would have to go to the concert with her. Then she mentioned that two of her best friends would be coming with us as well. These women were about ten or fifteen years older than me. I was used to that kind of age gap; after all, my best friend Gaye was ten years older than me and George was sixteen years older than me. But these women were "older" than me in a non-numerical way.

Cali told me that she and her girlfriends had not smoked pot since university and she asked if I could get them high for the concert. I said sure. When I mentioned it to George, he was adamant that I shouldn't do it. "Don't smoke weed with straight people, Candy, it will come back to bite you on the ass. Straight people will rat you out in the minute if anything goes wrong as well. They panic so easily." When George said "straight people," he was not talking about sexual preference. He meant people who have very conservative lives and narrow life experience. I told him he was crazy. It was just a little bit of weed, what could possibly go wrong? (Foreshadowing intended!)

The day of the concert rolled around and I had picked up ten grams of weed. I rolled a joint at home to take with us. I did ask George about how much to put in the joint. He said the last time these women had smoked, it was probably some homegrown stuff from the seventies. They wouldn't be used to this hydroponic weed, so I shouldn't put too much. I rolled the joint with mostly tobacco and sprinkled a little bit of weed in it. I picked everybody up in my car.

It was a beautiful August day in Halifax, and at 6:30 p.m., the city was awash in sun. I felt like it was going to be a great night.

As I drove around looking for a spot to park, I opened my car ashtray, took out the joint and lit it up. The three of them were tittering like old ladies at a bingo. "We can't smoke it right here. What are you doing?" I told them to chill out. It was going to take me a few minutes to find a place to park so we would smoke at the same time. I told them, "Just hold it like it's a cigarette, it's fine. No one is sticking their head into my car." The joint went around the car exactly twice. Then they said they'd had enough. So four of us smoked one half of one joint that had barely any weed in it to begin with.

I found a parking spot and we made our way, on foot, to the Metro Centre. As we were entering the centre, Cali told us that one of her clients worked for one of the presenting sponsors and they gave her a great ticket—really close to the stage . . . but there was only one primo ticket. The other three tickets were way up in the nosebleeds. I got very excited. I assumed she would give me the great ticket and she would sit with her friends, who I didn't even know. Of course not. She was taking the good ticket, and as a happy end-of-summer gift to me, I would be sitting with her friends in the nosebleeds.

I mentally rolled my eyes and started the long climb to our seats with her two friends. I didn't really have anything to say to these women, so I was anxiously waiting for the show to start. The opening act was a singer I didn't really know, so I sat patiently, waiting for it to be done while the friends chit-chatted. Finally, the lights dimmed and I heard the first few recognizable notes to one of my favourite songs. Out came Van Morrison. He was singing the first line of "Moondance" when all of a sudden, one of the women grabs my arm and says, "I'm having a bad trip. I have to get out of here."

A bad trip? What the hell was she talking about a bad trip? We didn't just drop acid. I told her, "You are not having a bad trip. We did not do acid. In fact, you barely did weed. There was a lot of tobacco in that joint, so you are probably feeling light-headed and maybe a little nauseous. So sit there and cool your jets and let me enjoy this concert."

Nope. She wasn't having it. She was positive she was having a bad trip and she needed ME to get her out of there. Why not her friend who was sitting right next to her? I realized I had to take her out or she was not going to let me hear this concert. I grabbed her by the arm, dragged her down the stairs and frog-marched her to the bathroom. In the bathroom, I splashed cold water on her face and then I took her to a bench just outside and sat her down. I spoke to her the way you speak to a six-year-old when you really want to make sure they understand. I was standing in front of her bent over with the index finger of my right hand in her face and gripping her arm with my left hand.

"Look," I said, "you are going to sit here and shut up and I am going to get Cali and she can deal with you. You are not going to talk to anyone until I get back with Cali. You are NOT going to tell anyone you smoked weed. I am about to start my third year of law school and I have ten grams on me, so you are going to sit here and shut up. Do you understand me?" With a stunned look on her face, she nodded that she understood.

I burned it out to Cali's seat, grabbed her and got back to the bathroom area in less than five minutes. As we were turning the corner to the bench, I saw two Halifax police officers and a paramedic circled around Cali's friend, and she was saying "I smoked some marijuana . . ." I stopped dead in my tracks. I told Cali, "You have to deal with this.

She said, "Yes, but my bag is in your car and they are taking her to the hospital." The *hospital*?! For two puffs on a joint?! And Cali tells me she wants me to drive her to the hospital. I made the long walk back to get my car, drove back to the Metro Centre to get Cali and brought her down to the hospital. And by the time I got back to the Metro Centre, the concert was just ending.

What a night. Oh, but that wasn't the end of it. This was the gift that just keeps on giving. Fast-forward five years. I was now working for the Nova Scotia government. My deputy minister was interested in an Indigenous training program I designed.

She said, "I am going to bring my friend over for a meeting because she is in charge of staff training for the government." My brain must have blanked that woman out of my memory because I didn't even recognize her face when she came to my office the next day.

I had the meeting, and that night I was in the car on the way home when all of a sudden, I had a flashback. I called Gaye and asked her, "What was the name of that dingbat who ruined the Van Morrison concert for me?" She told me and I knew it was her. The next day, I was attending a meeting she was at. I asked her to step out into the hall, and I said, "Do you know who I am?" She said yes. I said, "No, but do you know who I am in terms of the Van Morrison concert?"

"Well, yes, I freaked out when the deputy called me because I totally remember that story and I had to pay a bill for the ambulance that night and I hid it from my husband because I didn't want him to know I smoked weed." *Is he your husband or your father??!!* "So," she says, "when the deputy called me, I told her the whole story!"

She told my deputy minister that I got her high at a concert and she had to go to the hospital. When she saw that I was freaking out, she said, "Oh, it's okay, the deputy is one of my best friends." Well, she wasn't my friend. She was my deputy minister! My reputation was at stake. At that point, I had been separated from George for about three years, but I heard his wise words in my head: "Don't smoke weed with straight people." I have learned that lesson.

When I say I learned a lesson, I mean that in more ways than one. While this has become a very funny and very entertaining story, there is so much to mine from it on reflection. Why did they ask me to supply the weed to them? Would my boss have asked a white person from a well-to-do family to furnish her with weed? How casually this woman put my job in jeopardy when she shared the story with my deputy minister. That was the part that George was trying to get across, that "straight people," as he referred to them, see people like me as so expendable, they would throw me under the bus with such casualness.

In situations like this, loving yourself becomes so important, so that you can truly see the big picture. When I say this incident taught me a lesson, I mean that it taught me a lesson about them, not about me.

That was how my third year of law school started. I was in worse financial condition than I had ever been, but the end was in sight. I struggled my way through third year as I continued to gain weight. I ended up in the hospital that year for asthma and to have surgery on my sinuses. George and I fought and made up, fought and made up. There was drama with other women and drama around money. And deep down, I had not forgiven him for not taking me home when Billy died.

By the time I was within a month of the end of school, I was a mess. I had no money. There was no food in my apartment and I had to go to the food bank for some groceries to get me to the end of the year. The family was planning to come down for graduation. I was giving the valedictory address. My health was falling apart and so was my life. I thought that if I could just make it to graduation, everything would be great. I had a job waiting. A prestigious corporate firm had already made me an offer, and once I started working, everything would be okay. Boy, was I wrong.

The one where I meet some mean girls

All the hard and turbulent times I've described so far are still what I consider good times. I was young, free and, by and large, happy. The three years following law school graduation was the only time in my life when I was truly and thoroughly unhappy. My mom used to tell me to picture the person I wanted to be and make my decisions based on whether or not the choice would bring me closer or further away from that person. When I think about that, I realize that during the time at the firm, I completely lost sight of the person I wanted to be. She and I were estranged and it was a hard fight to get back to her.

On paper, it seems like this should have been a positive time. I had graduated from law school and was clerking at a corporate law firm, along with four or five other graduates from my class. Every television show or movie told me I should be happy. I wasn't.

Work at the firm started off on the wrong foot. Part of that was my fault and part of it was theirs. During my time in law school, I started getting media attention for various accomplishments. Being valedictorian brought recognition and I was interviewed a few times for TV news stories. I believe members of the partnership saw the potential in my media coverage and wanted me to further exploit that. I don't think the attention went over very well with the other associates and clerks.

One thing about my life is that I've always found it easy to make friends . . . I shouldn't say always, but mostly. Grade one was tough because I wasn't socialized yet. But as soon as I was, for my entire life, it was very easy for me to make friends. I was always liked by people. When I ran for president of my student council in grade twelve, there were eight hundred and fifty people in my school, and eight hundred of them voted for me. I was valedictorian of my law school graduating class. I've never had a hard time fitting in. I've made friends at every place I have ever worked, and to this day remain in contact with them. So, it was such a shock for me when I landed at that firm to find that I could not get people to like me.

At the time, I blamed them entirely. While I still feel that a number of those associates acted atrociously, in retrospect

I take some responsibility for not fitting in. It was years later, when bullying became part of the zeitgeist, that I realized I had in fact been bullied by the associates at that firm, while at the same time being favoured by some of the partners. It put me between a rock and a hard place.

But the first revelation I had about bullying was far more disturbing to me. I realized I had been a bully once. When I was eight years old, I had this new best friend, who I'll call Barbara, and for some reason, she and I decided that there was one girl in our class who we were going to torture. Sadly, she also happened to be my cousin Shelley. In grade three, we made her life hell. It embarrasses me even now, decades later, to think about it. Day in, day out, we just bullied and ridiculed my dear cousin Shelley for absolutely no reason. It was a constant verbal barrage.

After grade three it ended, but I don't remember a formal makeup. I just started talking to my cousin Shelley again. I know that I never apologized during all our years of school together. It took me until I was a full-grown adult to apologize to Shelley properly, and she was so gracious when I reached out to her. She said, "Grade three was a nightmare, but I forgave you for that long ago." I am so embarrassed of my behaviour. She told me, "We were eight years old, let it go." But I still feel shame for it even now. I never fully understood what it meant to be bullied and how painful it can be until I went to work at that firm.

For the first year after law school, your title is law clerk. During that year, you get experience in all areas of law and take your bar course, and at the end of that year, you take your bar exam. Law school basically teaches you how to use the law library. The year of clerking is supposed to teach you how to be an actual lawyer. Senior associates and partners give you assignments and you learn from your peers and the junior associates as you work through those assignments.

I feel that several lanes of my life went wrong during my time as a clerk.

In terms of the work, I remember on my first day there was a memo on my desk asking me to prepare a damage assessment for one of the senior litigation lawyers. She was a woman I liked as soon as we met. She was scrappy, smart and had a great sense of humour. I had no idea what a damage assessment was so I asked her about it. She told me to go to my peers. The problem was I didn't have peers to lean on. It was my feeling that many of the clerks and associates thought I had only been hired because I was Indigenous and I filled the firm's employment equity quota. I couldn't discuss those feelings with anyone because, with the exception of a very smart Chinese corporate partner who didn't seem to socialize with anyone, all my colleagues were white.

One of the paralegals kindly tried to help me, but when I passed the damage assessment in, the partner told me it was horrible. I was embarrassed, but I thought I would at least get feedback on it, which would help me for the next damage assessment. I knew I didn't want to work in litigation, but I did want to know how to do a damage assessment. When I asked in what way it was horrible, she simply said, "All of it." Since this was one of the few lawyers I really liked and felt liked me, it struck me in that moment that I was alone and would have to try to figure things out on my own.

I really do think she liked me, but I still don't understand why she didn't want to give me more constructive feedback on that damage assessment. It felt like striking out my first time at bat in a really important game, and it shook my confidence.

Meanwhile, I could tell I wasn't fitting in socially with the younger people at the firm, particularly the young women. As I said, I take responsibility for some of that. There is a very insular vibe at corporate law firms. In this case, the lawyers worked together, they socialized together and quite often they even bought houses in the same part of town. This makes sense, I guess, if you go right from high school to undergrad to law school and then into a firm. I had lived so much life and had a really tight group of friends, so I wasn't looking to socialize with these people outside of work. But I had hoped we could be friendly at work.

I was also having a cultural shock of sorts. I attended many of the social functions of the firm as was expected of us as clerks. They stressed "fitting in" and I realized I wasn't doing very well in that regard. It quickly became clear to me that a number of these lawyers had alcohol addiction problems. One of the lawyers was cheating on his pregnant wife, who I had met at social functions. I felt like such a heel knowing what I knew and just talking small talk to this poor woman. The environment was unhealthy.

It also shocked me how coddled some of these young lawyers were. They would be devastated if their free parking space was two blocks away from the building. One of the young associates had a total meltdown one evening because someone had taken her lunch out of the fridge. I mean a real meltdown. I was in my office when I heard the crying. She was in the hallway and some other lawyers were around her consoling her. I thought someone close to her had died. I stood there stunned when I realized all this was about someone eating her Lean Cuisine. Jesus, did these people have no sense of real turmoil? I thought of some of the people who I worked with at Tim Hortons, trying to raise kids on minimum wage and deciding between paying the rent or buying groceries. But for this privileged young woman, someone taking her lunch out of the fridge (ironically, a common occurrence I covered on my radio show years later) was a complete disaster to her.

Meanwhile, my weight was continuing to climb, and my fights with George were increasing. I wanted him to come to firm events with me. He kept telling me "those people" did not want someone who looked like him at their functions. I kept telling him they wouldn't judge him, that if they knew he was my partner, they would welcome him with open arms. This is another point he was right about. Having a partner like George was yet another element that separated me from the herd. I had moved from Tawaak housing to a small apartment in the

South End of Halifax. I was having trouble making the rent in this new apartment and I couldn't figure out how to catch up. It was putting more and more pressure on me, and I was so scared someone would find out how screwed up I was. Smack-dab in the middle of that clerking year, George got busted for having two ounces of weed in his car. The cop who busted him clearly didn't like the look of him because he impounded the car and was hell-bound to take him to court.

I was so scared the firm would find out, I reached out to a lawyer who was a friend from another firm. She agreed to take the case off the books. I didn't want people at her firm to know my partner was in this situation either, because she worked with the wife of a senior partner from my firm. I paid her in cash delivered to her house and then I paid to get George's car out of the pound. There went my rent money for that month.

In November of that year, I went with a handful of lawyers to a fundraiser for the Saint Mary's University hockey and football teams. I bid on and won a Huskies work crew. The idea was for eight of the Huskies players to come to your house and do any work you had to do, like mow the lawn and clean the gutters. When I placed the bid, it was because it was the only thing going cheap enough for me to afford. When I won, I knew instantly what work I wanted them to do. My thirty-first birthday was on December 4, and I told them they would be serving the food and booze at my party.

I told my friends, and we were all looking forward to it. The senior female lawyer who I liked knew about my plan, and she offered to host it at her house. She lived in a huge house and it would be easier to have it there than in my small apartment. I thought if I included some of the young women from the firm, and it was at the partner's house, then it might help me fit in. The associates who were rude to me asked if they could bring some friends to the party. I said yes, once again hoping this would ingratiate me to them. The party was a hit. The Huskies stripped down to their boxer shorts and served way too much tequila. My friends had a great time and I could tell people from the firm really cut loose. At the firm holiday party a few weeks later, one of those lawyers got up and talked about the party of the year (which I quickly realized was my party) and presented T-shirts to all the women from the firm who had been at the party . . . except me. I actually laughed as it was happening. It seemed so "high school" to me. Like a scene out of the movie *Mean Girls*. I was thirty-one years old and couldn't believe that educated grown-ass women conducted themselves in this way. I confronted the person who had presented the shirts and said, "It was my party that I invited you to. How could you not give me a T-shirt?" Her answer was that there simply were not enough shirts to give me one. They were cheap, white T-shirts they had bedazzled. I realized then how sheltered their lives had been and I lost all respect for them, which made me even less inclined to fit in.

I was doing a lot of public speaking at this time and most of it was being organized through the firm. I travelled to Prince Edward Island for one of the partners and spoke at a number of Rotary clubs. I was also being asked to speak at conferences all over the country. I wasn't charging for my speeches; I was travelling on firm time. The partners saw it as good media and I saw it as a great opportunity to get away from the environment that was taking such a toll on me.

At the end of my article year, the firm hired me as a lawyer. In the lingo of that business, it is called a "hire back." The hire-back rate for Mi'kmaq clerks in Nova Scotia was 0 percent . . . until me. This hire back was going to bring the firm a lot of publicity. It was a big deal. A glass ceiling was being broken. It was an important step in the process that began with the Donald Marshall Inquiry. Because of the weight of the situation, the firm threw a reception for me on the day I was called to the bar. Judges were invited, professors from the university were invited, key community people were invited. The media was there with television cameras. It was all very exciting.

Problem was, no other associate had been thrown a big, fancy reception on the occasion of being called to the bar. In advance, I thought this might be a problem and I discussed it with the senior partners I was close to. Those partners talked to the other associates and explained the historical significance of the occasion. It didn't matter. After that party, the handful of associates who I secretly dubbed the "mean girls" didn't even pretend to like me.

My life felt like hell. My relationship with George was growing more and more painful, and I knew I had to leave him or it was going to destroy me. He was the love of my life, though. He held me every night when I cried over how I was being treated at the firm. I would never have let anyone else know that these small-minded women were getting to me. At this point, the media was portraying me as a big success. In reality, I was getting ready to leave the love of my life, who I knew was bad for me. I was in a financial mess. After a lifetime of being fit and athletic, I was continuing to gain weight and didn't really know how to deal with this new body. I hated going to the office every day, and I was disconnected from the work I was doing. On top of all that, the mean girls decided they would pile on.

They would make plans as a group for any firm-sponsored event and deliberately exclude me. Had I actually liked them, it would have hurt more, but because I didn't like or respect them, it simply made me angry. I wasn't going to let that happen. I felt it was important for me to push in this way in order to make room for all Indigenous lawyers who would come after me. If I let them exclude me without a fight, it would make it even easier for them to exclude the next lawyer they deemed unworthy. They were not woke, and I knew I was not going to succeed in making them "wake up."

There was a fundraiser at a local restaurant for a women's shelter. All my friends were going, but I heard that some women from the firm would be going too. I thought I should at least try to play nice and go with the firm. I told the woman organizing the firm table that I wanted to go. She told me, "This isn't a firm-sponsored event. We bought our own tickets." I said,

"That's cool, I will pay for my own ticket." She at least had the decency to look a little uncomfortable as she said, "We don't want you to come with us." Now I didn't come from educated parents and we didn't have a lot of money or fancy connections, but if I had ever been that rude to someone, my mother would have disowned me. Apparently, these women were not taught kindness.

My mouth fell open, but I just said, "It's fine, I will just go with my friends as I had originally planned." As luck would have it, the firm table was right next to the table I was at with all my friends. The organizers had taped nylons underneath each chair as a free gift. At the beginning of the night, they announced that there wouldn't be enough pantyhose for everyone, so if you didn't want the pantyhose, they asked that we hand them in so they could be distributed to women who did want them.

The pantyhose under the chairs were all size large. They were packaged the way pantyhose were always packaged—wrapped around stiff, square cardboard and then encased in plastic, with sharp corners. At a quiet moment in the evening when there was a lull in the activity, one of the women from the firm yelled, "Hey, Candy! You can have my pantyhose. They are large. Way too big for me, but they might fit you." She flicked her pantyhose at me, and before I could register what was happening, ten pairs of pantyhose hit me in the face.

My friends at the table with me happened to be the women in charge of labour relations at Dalhousie University.

The firm I worked for had been hoping to lure them away from the firm they were using for their labour work at the time. Heather, one of those friends, was the director of labour relations, and she wrote a letter to my firm indicating that they would never bring their work to a firm where lawyers behaved this way.

I was a feminist and an anti-racist activist when I arrived at the firm. It would take a few years before I would come to understand how the world responded to fat people, and it would take me a few years after that to become the body-positivity advocate I am today. That evening at the SoHo restaurant in Halifax, Nova Scotia, was my first experience with body shaming. It wasn't from some uneducated dude in his mom's basement; sadly, it was from a group of well-educated grown women. One of them had a ten-year-old daughter at the time, and most of them have gone on to have children. I have often wondered if any of them feel shame for their actions. I wonder how they talk to their own children about bullying.

What I knew for sure after that night was that I had no interest in being associated with people like that for the next thirty years of my life. I sat awake in my living room all night. I couldn't continue to be around the lawyers of that firm and I couldn't continue to be with George. For me to be happy, for me to honour the love my parents had poured into me, I could not continue to allow anybody to treat me with disrespect. So,

I was going to have to figure out how to walk away from what most people would see as a dream job, and I was going to have to leave the love of my life. I started sketching out a plan. Little did I know, a one-week fling with a lawyer in Ottawa would be the catalyst for my year of change.

SCENE II

The one where I didn't have an exit strategy

The only thing that got me through my time at the firm was going on the road, speaking at conferences. I was speaking at one such conference in Halifax when I spotted a woman I had seen at an event a couple of years prior. It had been a typical rubber-chicken dinner followed by a band and dancing. As the band was playing, a very fit blonde woman in a pair of trousers, dress shirt and vest walked up to the band, pulled a harmonica out of her pocket and began to jam with the band. Full disclosure, whether you are my type or not, as soon as you are onstage with a musical instrument, I am interested. I leaned over to the friend I was with and said, "I'm not gay, but if I was, I'd go after her." Fast-forward two years and there I was in Toronto, speaking on a panel, and the blonde harmonica player was sitting next to me.

Her name was Leigh and we hit it off. We chatted for the rest of the night. I learned that she lived in Ottawa. As she drove me back to my hotel, I told her I would be in Ottawa the following week and asked if I should call her. She said yes. I realized I had a crush . . . on a woman. After I flew back from that trip, I was only home for less than twenty-four hours. I didn't see George in that time. I dumped the dirty underwear out of my suitcase, packed some clean clothes and headed back to the airport for my trip to Ottawa. I called my friend Catherine and told her I had a crush on Leigh and that I wanted Catherine to host me and Leigh at her house for some drinks. The night went exactly as I had planned. Leigh came back to my hotel room with me and we had a week-long fling.

When I arrived back home in Halifax, I realized that the distraction of Leigh was the very catalyst I needed to finally end things with George. I had known for close to two years that I had to leave him. He was never going to live up to my expectations of him. I loved him so much. But I knew, by then, that I could not love him into being another person. Although at the time, I had never heard the term "polyamory," I suggested that we have an open relationship. So he could continue to see other people, but so would I. I was appalled that I would ever suggest it. He would not entertain me seeing other people. Numerous times during our years together, I had dated or flirted with other people, sometimes because I was truly interested in the guy, sometimes because I was hurt or angry at George. Every single time resulted in him tracking the guy down and threatening him. He was an imposing man; it always worked. It baffles me how much time and energy he spent trying to keep me faithful to him. He followed me. He checked my voicemails. The most shocking moment for me came one sunny Tuesday afternoon. I was standing next to the bookshelf in my apartment, talking on my landline. As I was talking, I just happened to cast my eyes down to the phone jack behind the bookshelf. I noticed there was a little adapter plugged into the jack and there were two cords coming out of the converter. One of the cords led to the phone I was talking on. I quickly ended my call and followed the second cord. It went around the side of my bookcase that was hidden from view, and then the cord disappeared behind my books. I removed my books from the shelf, feeling like I had suddenly landed in a John Le Carré novel, and there on the shelf inside a rolled-up towel, I found a recording device. I knew in an instant what was happening. He was recording and listening to all my phone calls.

The part about all this that baffled me was how easily he could have kept me loyal to him. All he had to do was be a better man. Had he put as much time and energy into our relationship as he did in surveilling me, I would have stayed with him forever.

Upon arriving home from that trip to Ottawa, I emailed him and asked him to stay away from the apartment for a few days. I told him I wasn't breaking up with him but that I needed some time to think. He gave me that time. We went five days without seeing each other, which was the longest we'd ever gone without contact. On the fifth night, I was on the phone with Leigh at about eleven when I heard the apartment door open and close. Just as I hung the phone up, he came around the corner and our eyes met. It was the strangest I had ever felt around him. Something had changed. I had turned the corner. When I started to speak, I was shocked to hear a waver in my usually smooth voice. I was physically shaking as I said, "I can't be with you anymore." He was angry. At first, he tried to convince me to stay, then he told me he knew I was going to leave him because he read it in my journal. In the arguing that happened over the next hour, he told me he had been reading my journal for years. I thought I was going to be physically sick. It was such an invasion of privacy, a real breach of trust that went beyond listening to phone calls. But what really struck me was that for years, he had been reading about how much he was hurting me, and yet he was able to go right on doing it. That made it clear I was making the right decision.

Once the fight went out of him, he told me that during all the years we had been together, he felt as though he was just holding space until something better came along for me. How strange. He was the person who'd had multiple lovers, but he thought I was the one looking for something better than him. I realize now how important that statement was, though. Ultimately, I felt he did not have enough self-confidence to be with a woman like me, and he revealed it to me then. He was wrong, though; that was not how I felt. I loved him completely. In fact, I never again loved anyone as deeply as I loved him. I was young and inexperienced when we met, but he wasn't. I think he knew in the beginning what I finally knew in the end—that he couldn't make the climb with me. I had plans, big plans. I was going to have to leave him at base camp, sacrifice him, for the chance at making the summit.

In the days following, he figured out where Leigh was and sent her a threatening message. Then he started sending me emails, first trying to convince me to come back to him and then threatening me. He emailed that he would call my mom and tell her things about me or call the firm and embarrass me. My friends were telling me to change my locks or move apartments. I didn't do any of those things because I knew George. I responded to one of the threatening emails and told him he would not do any of those things because he loved me and I loved him. And I was right.

My mother was the first person I called because I knew she would be my soft place to fall. True to form, she didn't say, "I told you so," she didn't bad-mouth George, she just consoled me. I was so sad that he was mad at me, and I couldn't believe, after all we had been through, that we would never talk again. He was my closest friend and confidant. Despite his shortcomings, he gave me a lot of good advice over the years. We really loved being together. We liked the same kind of music and movies. There was such a strong connection between us. My mother assured me that he was hurt, and anger was his way of expressing it. She felt that once he got over the anger, we could still be friends. She told me she always liked him, and she believed that had I not met him when I did, I might have developed a problem with alcohol. "He got you out of the bars and stopped your partying ways" was how she put it. After she died (seventeen years after we broke up), my sister found a picture of George and me in my mom's purse. It was a picture from the very beginning, taken in my apartment on Allan Street in Halifax. In it, I am twenty, young and beautiful. He has no grey hair yet and we are holding one another. I guess she really did care for him.

Mom was right about him getting over the anger. Within a few months, we had settled into a sort of friendship. He tried a few times to initiate sex with me during that first year apart. I refused. I wanted to say yes so badly, but breaking up with him was the hardest thing I'd ever done. (The only thing harder is the struggle to lose weight, which I have not succeeded at.) Breaking up with him felt like getting over a drug addiction. Being able to meet for coffee from time to time was a form of methadone, but I knew if I crawled into bed with him, I would be right back down the rabbit hole. So I resisted the urge. About six months later, I met my wife (more on that later) and moved into her house way out in the countryside. George moved in with one of the other women he was seeing and got her pregnant within a year of our split. We continued to meet for coffee from time to time. And I often wondered if I might have made a mistake in leaving him. I stopped wondering about that on the day their child was born. He called me at work and asked if I wanted to go for a coffee. We met up and drove down to one of our old favourite spots by the water. I asked him why he was in town. He said she was in the hospital and might be having the baby later that day. Then he talked about what she looked like pregnant. He talked about seeing her standing by the tub with all of the weight she had gained in pregnancy and how disgusted he was with it. First of all, I had gained a considerable amount of weight at that point, so it was insulting to me. But this was so appalling. In that moment, I knew I had dodged a bullet.

It took me years to figure out that being cheated on had nothing to do with me; it had to do with the cheater. I remember when it was all over the news that Richard Gere cheated on Cindy Crawford. I had a revelation. Cindy Crawford was cheated on? That was the moment it dawned on me that cheaters cheat and it has nothing to do with any of the people they are involved with.

Before getting to this serenity about the long years I spent with George, there were some very hard times to slog through. After I broke up with him, I didn't go to work for a week. I didn't know if I had any vacation time left and I didn't care. I was gutted, and there was no way I wanted to be around the vipers at the firm while I was in this fragile state.

My personal life had imploded, my financial situation was still in a hangover from my time with George and now I had to deal with the fact that my professional life was going to need to change or I was likely going to die of a stress-related heart attack.

After the week off, I returned to work and was even more miserable than I had been before. I slogged along while I was also trying to figure out how to date women after my experience with Leigh. I had a lot of friends who were lesbians, but I didn't want to date them because I had known them forever. A friend suggested I try the internet. Now, that might sound perfectly normal as you read this. But, I remind you, this was 2001, and it was still considered pretty risqué to actually meet up with someone you found online. Still, I went to a web personals page and registered under "women seeking women."

The first thing I had to do was post a picture of myself. At that point, I was around a hundred pounds heavier than I had been when I started law school. My first-year law school composite picture was a great shot of me. I convinced myself that since the picture was not too old, it was fair game to post it. Then I had to fill in the profile information. In order to increase my chances of "bagging a lesbian," I entered things that I thought would be appealing to gay women. Oh, what a naive baby queer I was. I said I liked vegan cereal (I would eat steak seven nights a week if I didn't think it would kill me), Birkenstocks (I lived in spike heels), dogs (I am allergic to them) and hiking (at that point, I didn't even like walking anymore). And after filling in all those false facts, I hit send. Just like that, I had entered the brave new world of internet dating. I received some pics of women in bikinis, one of which was up on my computer screen at work when one of the managing partners came into my office to borrow a bag. Could things get any worse at work?

Then, after about two weeks, I received a one-line message from a person calling themselves CountryGal30: "I don't like computers, here is my phone number, call me if you want." It made me chuckle. I scribbled the number down in my day planner and then forgot about it. I left town for a week to speak at a couple of conferences. A few nights after returning home from that trip, I remembered CountryGal30. It was a Wednesday night at about eight when I called her. When she answered, I introduced myself, and the first thing she (very coldly) said was, "I sent you that message two weeks ago." Then she said, "My name is Denise." We talked until two o'clock in the morning. We shared a lot of the same values and she was very easy to talk to. She told me she was a registered veterinary technician who had graduated from St. Clair College in Ontario. She said she worked long hours at the clinic, but she might give me a call on Friday night when she got home from work.

My Friday nights had always meant meeting up with friends for a happy hour drink after work. I was usually the last person to leave happy hour. That Friday night, I threw some money on the table at 7:00 p.m. and flew out of there like my pants were on fire. My friends would tease me about that for months to come, but I didn't want to miss her call. We spoke on the phone until midnight, at which point, she said, "You know I have to work at seven thirty, but I could drive into the city right now to see you." That was a forty-five-minute drive she was willing to make. I looked around at the ketchup bottle in the middle of the floor and last week's panties hanging off a rubber tree plant and realized I couldn't let her in my apartment. I told her to buzz me from the lobby and we would take a drive down to Point Pleasant Park. I hung up, feeling excited, and then I remembered . . . the picture. She was expecting to find 165-pound Candy, but 235-pound Candy was about to meet her at the door.

Well, I figured, there was nothing I could do about it then. She arrived at about one, and when I opened the door, she looked at me from head to toe and then asked when I had taken the picture on my profile. I told her I looked different because the photo was black and white. We went to the park and talked until the sun came up and she had to go to work. We had our first kiss, which was terribly awkward. My tongue was pierced and she was scared to death to touch the barbell I had in it at the time. She went to work and I went home and slept the day away. I did mention to her that I was going to a party at a friend's house and then I'd be heading down to a bar called NRG afterward. I didn't think there would be any chance she'd see me that night after being up the night before and then working all day. But she was a trooper. She got off work, had a nap at a friend's house and then came to NRG. I'm so glad she did because, having no idea of the tragedy that would follow, I was able to introduce her to my dear friend Darryl.

SCENE 12

The one where I up and quit the law

When I was working at the Tim Hortons on Quinpool Road, there were three gay men working there who were from Cape Breton. There was a tall, skinny guy named Bruce, an edgy artistic guy named John and John's boyfriend, Darryl. Darryl was the son of a butcher from Bras d'Or on Cape Breton Island. Darryl was beautiful. He had the deepest blue doe eyes and dirty-blond hair. He was so kind and sweet. We hit it off as soon as we met. I leaned on Darryl a lot during my hard times with George. One year, George and I were fighting around my birthday and Darryl threw me a birthday party at his place. We were inseparable for a couple of years, and then when I started law school, we lost touch for a while. I didn't have a social life at all while I was in law school, so I sort of lost touch with everyone.

During my articling year, Darryl worked at the Sobeys near my place. He would often pick up a six-pack of beer after work and come over. We would listen to music, talk about boys and share our dreams for the future with one another. On that Saturday night at NRG, as soon as I walked in the door, there was Darryl on the dance floor. He loved to dance. Later in the evening, I introduced him to Denise and we all danced together for a while. Before Denise and I left, I gave him a big hug and kiss and told him to call me. That would be the last time I ever saw him. He had asked me if I was going out the next weekend, but I told him I wanted to spend time with Denise. He went out with some friends to a bar called Reflections, then decided to stay at the bar after his friends left. A bouncer reported that he left the bar around midnight by himself. There is another report that he was seen around 2:00 a.m. on Gottingen Street in Halifax, running in the direction of the Macdonald Bridge. And then he vanished into thin air.

Thankfully, I was with Denise when this happened. She completely understood my frustration with how his disappearance was being handled. But more importantly, Denise is a very supportive person. She was, during that time of my life, a soft and safe place to land, as my mother had been for me in the past, which made dealing with Darryl's disappearance a bit easier.

Despite the efforts of his parents and friends, then and over the years, there have been no clues to Darryl's whereabouts or what happened to him. His mother never did recover from it and died in her sixties, presumably of a broken heart. Last year I provided the court with an affidavit in order to help Darryl's father have him declared dead.

At least once a month, I scan John Doe websites and search the internet in hopes of finding something relevant. Every time the news reports that human remains have been found, my heart stops. I pray that his father will know what happened to Darryl before he dies and I have that same hope for myself. Darryl was a kind, caring person. He was a great friend. I've included his missing-person information at the end of this book in hopes that someone, somewhere, knows something.

I was so happy to have been able to introduce Darryl and Denise because, as it turns out, from that first weekend we met, Denise and I have never been apart. You may be wondering about all those fibs I wrote in my online bio. Well, they did come back to bite me. On that very first weekend, I found myself at Denise's house out in the country preparing for a hike. She suggested that, since we were both "experienced hikers" (NOT), we hike in the woods behind her house instead of on a trail. The only sneakers I owned were big white volleyball sneakers. She looked at them sort of funny as we started our hike. I asked her to go in front of me since I didn't know the area. In reality, I just didn't want her to see me fall if I tripped. We set out and it was a nightmare from the get-go. The blackflies were eating me alive. I felt like I was snorting them up my nose . . . which was running because of my allergies to most things outdoors. Meanwhile, my long hair was getting caught in the branches and it was sticking to my heavily glossed lips. As I swiped at that hair to get it out of my mouth, it was dragging lip-gloss whiskers across my face in every direction. I struggled through it all while thinking, "Don't let her see me fall, don't let her see me fall." And that's when it happened. The toe of that big white court shoe caught on a root and . . . timber!!! Down I went. My only saving grace was that she was in front of me. Alas, she turned around just in time to see me bounce off the forest floor. She obviously felt sorry for me, as she helped me up and suggested we head back to her house.

That story has become a part of my stand-up. Years later, as Denise's fortieth birthday approached, I asked her what she wanted. She asked for a tattoo on her arm from a prominent portrait tattoo artist. I was flattered that she wanted a portrait of me. I started looking through my glossy publicity shots. She stopped me and informed me she would be tattooing the picture of me that I'd advertised and she'd never got! Sure enough, right on her left biceps is a tattoo of twenty-five-year-old me!

From that weekend on, we have been a dynamic duo. It wasn't that crazy kind of lose-your-mind love. It felt sturdy and reliable and we were really good friends. We have reinvented our marriage many times in the twenty years that we have been together. There is a moment in the first Twilight movie when Bella's father tells her she will have to learn to love what's good for her. Denise is what's good for me. But, before we got to the happily-ever-after, there were some challenges.

When I met Denise, she was earning about $27,000 a year as a vet technician. I was a lawyer working in a corporate firm. I was moving out of my apartment, and she suggested I move in with her "temporarily" until I found a new place. So I moved my mountains of clothes and "stuff" into her small one-bedroom house, which overwhelmed her. Then, during my first week there, I emptied the well. I grew up on spring water. I didn't know anything about a well. I got up one morning, took a bath and then did two loads of laundry. Oops. She was very nice about it. I was still crying over George a lot, and she was okay with that, too. But I was harbouring a secret that I feared she would not be okay with. I hated my job and wanted to quit. No, I didn't want to quit—I felt like I needed to quit or I would have a full-on nervous breakdown.

I didn't have an exit strategy, and for one of the few times in my life, I didn't know what I was going to do next. And even stranger, I didn't feel that I had the energy to try to figure it out. I just wanted everything to stop. I didn't plan when or how I was going to do it. I just walked into the firm one morning, passed a couple of the "mean girls" in the hall, felt the cold shoulder, walked into my office and looked down at the work on my desk, which not only didn't interest me but actually disgusted me. I had been a union supporter and activist all my life and continue to be now. But at the time, I was working in a labour law group that represented management. I dropped down into my chair and felt that the weight of the world was on my shoulders. Without even thinking about it, I picked up the phone and called the guy in the labour group who had just made partner and who I liked a lot. I asked him to come to my office. He came in and I said, "I would like to walk out of this office right now and never come back, but I'm broke. You know and I know this isn't working. I would like to leave quietly but with a cheque in my pocket." I told him I would come back on the weekend to pack my office because I didn't want to see any of those women again. He spoke to the managing partners, and about forty minutes later, I walked out, cheque in hand, got in my car, drove back out to the house in Rawdon and told Denise I was unemployed.

I hadn't thought about what I was going to tell my parents or my friends. I didn't know what I was going to do to support myself, but I knew I had made the right decision because it felt like a massive weight had been lifted off my shoulders. For the next six months, the rumour mill in Halifax flew. I heard everything: that I had been disbarred, that I had stolen money and that I had had an affair with one of the senior lawyers . . . just a litany of rumours. I felt so destroyed. I ran into a senior lawyer who I had been close to at the firm. He made direct eye contact with me and quickly just turned his head away, pretended like he didn't see me. That stung.

For a year, I did not work. For a year, I did not see my friends. For a year, I did not even go into the city. I stayed in Denise's house in Rawdon. I would get up in the morning, make toast and coffee, and she would go to work and I would read a book. I always have way more books than I'll ever read. I buy more than I can ever read. In fact, if I stopped buying books right now, I probably wouldn't be able to finish all the books I own before I die. That year in Rawdon was the only time in my life when I could read every book I owned. And that's what I did. I just read every day. At the end of the day, I would make supper and have it ready for when Denise came home. There were a lot of tears during this time, but I really needed that year. Sometimes you have to give yourself the time to heal before you start rebuilding.

Since leaving the firm, I have only talked publicly about this experience twice. Once at the microphone when I was hosting an event, I talked about bullying in the workplace, and I revealed that I had gone through it. And then I never spoke about it again until right now, dear reader, in this book. What I think is amazing about this part of the story, though, is that it has become the best thing that ever happened to me. Because I would not have left the firm if those women hadn't been so damn mean to me. No matter how much I hated the work, if I had made friends there, I likely would have stayed. I likely would have found myself way further down the road in a career that did not give me any joy, doing work that I wasn't passionate about and missing the actual gift that I had, missing what my actual role in life was meant to be. So, by quitting my job at the firm and taking the time to deal with my feelings, I had prepared myself for the next step. And what a step it was.

I had always felt like my life would be spent in the public eye, but I wasn't sure what shape that would take. As a high school student, I had known how great it felt to be at centre court with an audience cheering me on. The larger the crowd, the better I played. For a while, in high school, I thought my path would take me into politics. Although I have been approached by two different parties on numerous occasions to run both provincially and federally, grown-up Candy knows politicking is not her game. I knew I wouldn't find my way to the stage through music because I had no musical ability. I did a lot of public speaking from the time I was a child. I loved it. But it hadn't dawned on me that I could earn a living with it.

When I went to law school, I set aside thoughts of a public life and accepted that law would be my path. At thirty-two, after breaking down in every way possible, I was out in the country with all this time to think, to reflect on my life and to plan. Once I started healing and feeling stronger, I put a plan together. I like to call it my plan for world domination. But, before I tell you that, I should tell you a bit more about the transition from spending years with a man to starting a new life with a woman.

SCENE 13

The one where I make
the best decision

When I'm asked to give young women advice, I have one piece that I always put at the top of the list: "Choose your partner wisely." Society as it was constructed when I was in my early twenties, and even now to some extent, favours a man's drive for the top. It favours a man's ambition. When a woman gives up her career ambitions to support her male partner in the pursuit of his career, no one questions it. It isn't quite so easy, as a woman, to find a male partner to give up his ambitions for yours.

I've had a partner for the past twenty years who has been picking up my slack as I continue to run down this dream. That partner is my wife, Denise. My relationship with Denise is complicated, beautiful and key to the story. But before I get into the nitty-gritty of our partnership, I should go back and talk about my early experiences with boys and men that eventually led me to the woman with whom I did something I thought I would never do . . . get married.

Long before I ever thought about serious life decisions, I was a kid with crushes, like everyone else. I had discovered aspects of my sexuality very young but didn't realize it was related to crushes on boys.

For me, the joy of sex started before I knew what sex was. Starting at five years old, I discovered that if I sat on the edge of the couch, held my breath, squeezed my thighs together really hard and rocked back and forth, I would experience this little explosion of euphoria. I used to call it "doing my thing."

It would anger me to no end if I was in the middle of "doing my thing" on the living room couch and my mom came in and stopped me before the rush of euphoria happened. Mommy didn't tell me it was sexual; she told me I shouldn't do it because holding my breath destroys my brain cells. I guess that was marginally better than telling me I would go blind. Either way, five-year-old me could not believe that something that felt this good could be bad for you, so I got savvy and started doing it more privately where no one would catch me. And more importantly, where no one would stop me.

I had no idea it was sexual in any way. Then, when I was in grade eight, I bought *Mademoiselle* magazine for the first time. It is no longer in print, but that was the beginning of my lifelong love of magazines. Even in this digital age, I am subscribed to about eight different magazines and I love it when they land in my mailbox each month.

At the time, I liked *Seventeen* magazine, but reading *Mademoiselle* made me feel so grown up. One Saturday afternoon, I came across an article in the magazine entitled "The Big O." Comically, I thought it was going to be about the Olympic stadium in Montreal. The article, as it turns out, was about orgasm, and it stated that some women could reach orgasm by pressing their thighs together. Although I was all alone in my room, my face turned bright red. I realized that "doing my thing" was masturbating.

When we are young, I think we all assume our parents know nothing about sex, so although I was a bit embarrassed to have figured out what I was doing, I wasn't too worried about it because obviously my parents didn't know what masturbation was. Oh, the bliss of being young and naive.

I really never gave it another thought; then, when I was twenty-five, my mom was visiting me in Halifax. We were on our way to an event in my car, Mom in the passenger seat and three of my friends in the back seat. I can't remember what we were talking about, but my mom suddenly said, "Remember when you used to masturbate when you were five and you called it 'doing your thing'?" Nice timing, Mom. My friends teased me about that for years.

When I think back to those young years, however, I really didn't relate "doing my thing" to the crushes I had on boys . . . or should I say men. The first crushes I remember having were on some of the bikers who came to the shop. That was where my love of men with long hair and beards began. The pimply faced boys at school weren't all that interesting to me until I was in high school. But even then, while some of the boys in high school were kind of cute, none of them really drew my attention.

I spent a lot of time and energy on my athletic pursuits as well as student council and the numerous other things I was involved in, so it didn't leave a lot of time for chasing boys. But also, I wasn't interested in dumbing myself down or being less competitive for the sole purpose of making some boy feel more comfortable, which it seemed like other girls were doing. Then (and now), I always needed to be the one in charge. I don't think that trait is particularly endearing to teenage boys. So although I dated, I never really got very serious about any boys. Full disclosure, however: there were a couple of teachers and a few of my friends' dads that I had huge crushes on. One was my English teacher Mr. Lushington. That crush was so big I took a train from Dalhousie, New Brunswick, to Halifax, Nova Scotia, on my high school March Break to go and read his master's thesis on John Keats at the Killam Library at Dalhousie University. I've spoken about that crush so often that last year, when I travelled home to celebrate the birthday of my former principal and dear friend Sandy MacLean and I introduced

Mr. Lushington to Denise, she said, "Oh wow, the famous Mr. Lushington." How embarrassing. (P.S., even in his seventies, Mr. Lushington has still got it.)

I had no interest in losing my virginity while I was still in high school. There were two pretty powerful reasons for that. I had grown up hearing the word "squaw" a lot. It was a word used synonymously with slut when referring to Indigenous women. I never wanted any of the guys I went to high school with to use that word against me, and I also never wanted any of them to feel superior to me. Disrespect is something I have always had a problem with. Even now, it doesn't bother me if someone doesn't like me or disagrees with me, but I can't tolerate it when someone disrespects me.

The only thing, at that age, that scared me more than being disrespected was disappointing my parents. It was particularly easy to disappoint my father. I figured out, at a very young age, that being a girl automatically put me at a higher risk of doing that, and I knew a lot of that was tied to sexuality. Being a "good girl" in my father's eye was important to me and was also a lot of work.

It's ironic that I finally lost my virginity to a boy from my hometown, but not until after I had graduated from high school. Christopher, as I mentioned in early chapters, was smart, athletic, had a razor-sharp wit and wasn't intimidated by strong or tall women. His life partner is a woman one inch taller than me who happens to be a judge . . . so he is the real deal, a completely secure man. To this day, he is one of my closest friends. I'm very proud of the fact that both my prom dress (a cocktail-length little black dress) and my first love stood the test of time. At fifty-two years old, I could still proudly go out on the town with both of them!

The first real adult relationship I had was with George. As I mentioned earlier, my sexual relationship with George was fantastic. In fact, I think I stayed with him many years longer than I should have because I didn't want to let go of that great sex. So it wasn't as though I had been living a lie until I started dating women. I had great and fulfilling sexual relationships with men. However, I always felt like I was in a power struggle with them. And I always wanted more, emotionally, than I seemed to be getting from men. I think the fundamental problem is that the kind of men I am attracted to sexually have dominant personalities, but I need to be the dominant person in my relationships. I think that was always a bit of a recipe for disaster.

With Denise, I knew I wouldn't have to worry about those things. I could be dominant and I would get what I needed emotionally. But I wasn't sure what "label" to choose because I still had a physical attraction to men. I didn't want to refer to myself as a lesbian because I felt that it disrespected Denise's life experience. When someone finds out they have Indigenous ancestry six generations back, they sometimes will say "I am Indigenous," which is very painful to people with lived experiences. Well, I had dated happily, no social pressures, no awkwardness around being asked if I had a boyfriend. Denise's life was the opposite of all that. She did struggle with knowing she was gay ever since she could remember and thinking she was the only person in the world who felt that way. So, I have always felt more comfortable referring to myself as queer.

Put whatever label on it you want; but when you fall in love with someone of the same sex and decide to make a life with that person, there is a process of coming out that is required. I let some of my closest friends know, then my family, and eventually I started to talk about her publicly in interviews and comedy material. One of the advantages of being a comedian is being able to work through life's challenges onstage.

When Denise and I met, it wasn't the same kind of feeling I had when I fell in love with George. It wasn't that red-hot physical attraction, but I wanted to be with her all the time. For the longest time, that confused me. I was scared of hurting her and was having trouble figuring out my own feelings, so I kept telling her that I couldn't commit to her long-term. I have always remained physically attracted to men, but Denise and I have something special, and I thought we both recognized it early on.

She was patient with me. She held me while I cried over George for the first year of our time together. She supported me financially as I took that year to heal from both George and my time at the firm. When I finally felt strong enough to get back on my feet and I started working again, I thought I should make a break from Denise. I had met a man I was interested in. He was African Nova Scotian, and we both did a lot of anti-racist work and met in that environment. I broke up with Denise and he and I had a brief affair. The affair was lovely; I still have a lot of warmth and respect for him. We both have huge egos, so I was pretty sure it would not be able to last. But it was lovely. The whole time I was still living at Denise's house in Rawdon. She, however, had cut me off (affectionately) when I had made the break. I was supposedly looking for an apartment of my own. She came with me to look at places, and she disapproved of all of them. At home, I cooked for her and put my cozy touches all around her house. Eventually, she told me it seemed like I didn't really want to be apart from her. She was right. At that point, I committed to Denise fully. We reunited and we put her little house in Rawdon up for sale and bought our first house together.

Denise and I have the most open communication between us. Over twenty years, we have gone through a few rough patches, but we have defined, for ourselves, what our relationship looks like. I chose the word "queer" because it feels the most appropriate to me.

Denise has been so good for me. And I have been good for her. We have been one another's therapist. We have been one another's life coach. And when my physical problems started limiting what I could do, Denise became, in many ways, my caregiver. We built *The Candy Show* brand together.

We both agree, however, that one person can't fulfill all of our needs. We have an open marriage and we have reworked the terms of our union many times over the past twenty years.

The one thing we always agree on is that we want to move forward together in whatever way works for us. Just like in my career choices, I don't spend much time worrying about what other people think a good marriage is. We define for ourselves what our partnership looks like.

SCENE 14

The one where
my dreams begin

Before I get to the plan I developed in that little house in Rawdon, I want to take one more detour back to my childhood and explain how I discovered my love of the spotlight.

As I mentioned in previous chapters, I was incredibly shy as a child, so my parents put me in majorettes hoping it would teach me how to socialize. The first time I ever stood on a stage was because of the majorettes. Once, when we were having a fundraiser, my friend Louise Upton and I got dressed up as old ladies and told a few jokes. Not original jokes we had written, just a couple of old chestnuts. When I launched the first joke, I was rewarded by laughter and applause. It felt great.

Years later, my mother told me how proud she was to see me stand in front of all those people (something she could never do). And she was happy that I was finally coming out of my shell. My family kids around about pushing me back into that shell, but back then, they were all pretty worried about me socially because I was so shy and had such difficulty being around strangers outside the family. So, this really was seen as a triumph.

In grade six, Mrs. Smissart held these wonderful drama sessions on Friday afternoons. We would dress up and act out various scenes. Some of them were comedy skits or dramatic scenes we wrote ourselves; sometimes it was a scene from a sitcom of the day, like *Three's Company.* I would borrow clothes from my sisters-in-law, who were small women, so by grade six, I could almost fit into their clothing. It was so fun to put makeup on, do my hair and act out these scenes in the little annex that was attached to our classroom. I looked forward to those Friday afternoons all week. Mrs. Smissart was very encouraging. At the end of the year, she told me she thought I had natural talent and she suggested I try out for drama the next year when I entered junior high.

I took her advice and tried out. I didn't even get a background part! The same thing happened in grades eight and nine. After three years, I accepted defeat and turned my attention to athletics. I thoroughly enjoyed my athletic life and I excelled at it. But I still felt like I was missing out on something that was meant to be. I used to go to school plays and variety shows and covered them in my weekly column in the town newspaper, the *Dalhousie News*. I loved showcasing the artistic expression of my fellow students, but I knew that I was an artist, too. I just didn't know how I would come to express that creativity.

From the time I was a little girl, I had dreams of being a ballerina. I had ballerina posters on my wall and jewellery boxes with tiny ballerinas inside that turned to the theme song of *Love Story*. The candle holders on my birthday cakes were little plastic ballerinas. When I was in grade three, Aloyse gave me a Ballerina Barbie as a gift. I still have her. Once a year, at Christmas, if I got the tinfoil just right on the rabbit ears, I could see a ballet performance on CBC. Everywhere I went, I didn't walk, I leapt through the air toward my destination. I was sure I looked as beautiful and graceful as those ballerinas I saw on TV.

Of course, there was no place in my hometown to take lessons. But then, when I was thirteen, a woman came to town who taught gave tap and ballet. My parents scraped together enough money to pay for the lessons and a leotard from the Sears catalogue. I was so excited. My friend Sheila and I were going to take the classes together. I always expected I would be much taller because at the age of thirteen, I was already about five feet, eight inches. I was all legs and arms. Although I was taller than everyone else, Sheila and I were the only two kids in the class. The rest were grown women. At one of the first lessons, the teacher was showing us how to do an arm movement. She turned around just as I was trying the movement with my long arms. She laughed, and in front of the whole class, she said, "You are supposed to do it gracefully, not like a big awkward dodo bird." I was mortified.

I took the rest of the classes that we had paid for, but I realized then that I would need to keep my dreams of being a dancer to myself. I am a strong believer that we should always have our eyes open wide when it comes to our dreams, because sometimes they come to us differently than the way we imagined. So, I protectively tucked my dream of dancing away for a couple of years. Then, when I was in grade nine, my parents, who had never mingled outside our family in my entire life, joined the Dalhousie Golden Age Club. The main activity for the Golden Age Club was Friday night dances. My parents announced that they, along with a bunch of other senior citizens, would be taking dance lessons. They would be learning the waltz, fox trot and jive. It wasn't ballet, but it was dance. So I asked my parents if I could go to the lessons with them. Without a word to my friends, every Wednesday night, I was learning the basic moves of ballroom dancing with a bunch of old folks.

All through high school, I would often tell my friends I had to be home early on Friday nights, but instead of going home, I would sneak over to the Golden Age Club and enjoy a few spins around the floor with my dad. His head used to come to my shoulders, but we both enjoyed those dances together. I thought to myself, This is how my ballerina dream is finding its way to me. At least I get to dance on Friday nights in a spot where no one is going to make fun of me.

In my first year of university, I found out the Royal Winnipeg Ballet was coming to the Fredericton Playhouse. I mentioned it to my mom on the phone, and a week later, the money for a ticket arrived in the mail. I got dressed up in my best outfit and went to see live ballet for the first time. I cried. It was even more beautiful than I imagined it would be. That night, I reformulated my dream. The new dream was to earn enough money in my life to be able to go to the ballet whenever I want. That dream came through. I have been enjoying live ballet for decades.

When my mom was eighty, she was visiting me in Halifax at the same time the Royal Winnipeg Ballet was performing at the Rebecca Cohn Auditorium. I bought us front-row seats and surprised her with them. That night, they began their performance with a very colourful contemporary piece. It was incredible to watch Mommy's face light up. I think I watched her more than the dancing that night. At intermission, she turned to me with tears in her eyes and told me how overwhelmed she was by this experience. I told her that was the gift she gave me all those years ago. Before multiple strokes made mobility a challenge for her, I exposed her to all the art I could. We saw a performance of *Cats* where one of the cats pounced on the arm of her chair and she giggled like a schoolgirl. After we saw Neptune Theatre's production of *Beauty and the Beast*, the entire cast came to meet her and take pictures with her in their costumes, thanks to my friend artistic director Jeremy Webb. My mother looked at Belle the same way I used to look at the ballerina in my jewellery box, like she was the most beautiful sight she had ever seen.

I was very content with the new iteration of my ballet dream. Since moving to Toronto, I've enjoyed multiple performances per year by the National Ballet of Canada. But as I said, you must keep your eyes open because your dreams don't always come to you the way you want them to. In the year I turned fifty, Denise, in her capacity as my manager, called me while I was away on a gig and told me to sit down. "The National Ballet," she said, "wants you to guest star as a Cannon Doll in this year's production of *The Nutcracker*." It was as if a silent movie of all the iterations of my dance dreams started playing in my head, going back in time to the little girl with a room full of ballet posters. I was in the middle of a conference centre, at a gig, but still I cried.

On Christmas Eve, 2019, fifty-year-old me, overweight and with arthritis, walked out, cane and all, on the stage at the Four Seasons Centre with the National Ballet of Canada. It was a five-minute part, but let me tell you, I lived a lifetime in those five minutes. I really took it all in. I took the time to look out at that audience and around the stage at all the dancers. Little girl Candy was losing her ever-loving mind! I didn't get to meet Karen Kain, but nonetheless, I was in HER production of *The Nutcracker*. Full circle ballerina-dream moment!

Keep your eyes open, dear reader, you never know how or when your dream will come to you.

But I digress. I was telling you how I came to my life in show biz. Well, after those stutter starts in dance and drama, I tried my hand at music. Daddy bartered for a little Como acoustic guitar by fixing a guy's bike, and they put me in lessons. After a couple of years of struggling through exciting numbers like "Down in the Valley" and "Hang Down Your Head Tom Dooley," I realized I was not going to be the next Liona Boyd.

While I was casting around trying to find my art, I kept finding myself speaking at a podium. It happened in small ways, like in my early student council days at school assemblies. It happened when the town was making presentations to the provincial government to have a sports complex built in Dalhousie, and I spoke on behalf of students. But I remember the first time I felt powerful doing it.

I was the president of the student council in grade twelve. Our school was geographically divided. One section housed academic classes and the other wing was for commercial classes. In other words, classes that were required by universities and classes for folks who planned to enter a trade or community college. I had strong support all over the school. A majority government, if you will.

The summer before, renovations were happening at the school. They finished the repairs on the academic side before school started. The repairs on the commercial side continued after school began. It meant a lot of noise and construction dust for the students in that wing. One afternoon, some cement that had spilled on the drop ceiling fell through and landed on a student's desk. That was the straw that broke the camel's back. They'd had enough.

I was sitting in Physics class when we all heard a loud noise that sounded like it was moving down the hall toward our classroom. Suddenly, the classroom door opened and a group of about twenty students were standing there. One of them said, "Candy Palmater, we voted for you, so you have to do something about this. Come with us and help." I looked at Mrs. Smith, our teacher, and she said, "Don't look at me, go with them." When we got down to the front lobby, I could see there were hundreds of students outside on the grass, gathered around the flagpole. My principal (and my mentor and friend, even now), Mr. MacLean, came out of his office with a bullhorn. He pushed it into my hands and said, "You have got ten minutes to get them back in here or I will have to call the police."

I went out and talked to them and convinced them to come back into the lobby—not class, just the lobby. Then I told Mr. MacLean he would have to sit down with us and hear their concerns and that we would have to come up with a solution together. It worked. Crisis averted. The event was covered by the *Dalhousie News* and there was a picture of me addressing the crowd.

At the time, I had a feeling this was a significant moment, but I wasn't sure what I was meant to take from it. As the years went by and I was asked to do more and more public speaking, the message was starting to take form.

One great thing that came out of my time at the law firm was my association with Big Brothers Big Sisters. One of the partners at the firm volunteered his time with them and he brought me to a board meeting. I really liked what they were doing in the community, so when they asked me, I joined the board. This was a very active group that held a lot of events and fundraisers. As usual, I found myself with a microphone in hand at many of the events. A large part of their fundraising each year was an event called Bowl for Kids' Sake. Different organizations in town would put teams together and raise money, and it all culminated in a big bowling weekend. To kick off the campaign, they usually hosted an event at one of the bars in Halifax. Ed Saunders, one of the employees at Big Brothers Big Sisters, was a musician and a theatre man. He and I started hosting the kickoff events.

For the first one, I just wore my usual clothes. But my cohost Ed was really fun to play with, and he recognized my comedic side and played the straight man for me. I would be about four years into my entertainment career before I realized how valuable that was, and I have been forever grateful to him. At those events, I began, safely, exploring my comedic side. The audience loved it. I wasn't delivering any preplanned material. I was just riffing and using my wit. I was being showered with laughter. The next year, I showed up in a zebra safari suit, and the year after that, I went all out and showed up in a full-on

Vegas-style white jumpsuit, complete with cape, my version of an Elvis outfit. I had it custom made for me. It was quite a hit with the crowd!

When I found myself out in Rawdon and nearing the end of my "lost year," I continued to be part of these Big Brothers Big Sisters events and I kept thinking about how it felt when I was onstage. I knew that I would not be able to support myself as an entertainer, particularly because I wasn't sure what exactly that was going to look like. So, first things first, I needed to find a job. I will forever be grateful to Denise for supporting us both on the $27,000 she earned that year, but it was time for me to get back into the workforce. I had let my bar fees lapse, mostly because I just didn't have the money to pay them, and because at that point, I was 90 percent sure I didn't want to practise law ever again.

I started applying for jobs with the provincial government. I was brought in for an interview with the Office of Aboriginal Affairs as a policy analyst. I got the job. But I wasn't out of the woods of my lost year yet. Shortly after moving in with Denise, something went wrong with my car. It wouldn't start and I couldn't afford to fix it, so I parked it in her yard and that is where it sat for the better part of a year. A mechanic who lived down the road asked me what was wrong with it. I told him I had no idea but I couldn't afford to fix it. He told me he would tow it to his place and try to figure out what was wrong because it wasn't good for the car to just sit there. Having grown up in a family of mechanics, I'm embarrassed to tell you this, but it was out of gas. That is all that was wrong with it. He called me and told me that, and then he asked me if I was interested in selling it. I took him up on the offer and sold the car. The money helped us through a few months. But when I got the job with the government, we only had one vehicle, Denise's Kia Sportage. My office was in downtown Halifax and I was working eight to four, Monday to Friday. Denise worked at the animal hospital out in Sackville and she worked split shifts.

Every morning we would get up at four and head into the city. On days when she worked twelve to eight, she would drop me off at the office and kill time until her shift started at noon. I would get off at four and kill time until her shift ended at eight. She'd pick me up at eight thirty, we would get back out to Rawdon by nine thirty. It was hard going. I didn't want to buy a car yet, because I was trying to pay off old debts. We started talking about putting the house in the country up for sale and looking for something in town.

In the meantime, another part of my plan was coming together. The year before I left the firm, my friends and I started attending a breast cancer support event called Titz'n Glitz. The first time I went, I saw that there was a photographer onsite taking pictures of some of the women wearing costumes for the purposes of a calendar that would be sold after the event.

When I'd seen the calendar the year before, I put a plan together in my head. I wanted to come up with an outfit that I thought would entice the photographer to include me in the calendar. If I could get myself in the calendar, somehow,

I would try to use the calendar as a springboard. My friends always put a theme together for the outfits they wanted to wear to the event. For the upcoming event, we all decided to dress up as cancan girls. Of course I wasn't going to be able to find a corset to fit me, so I had my friend Maureen custom make a purple and pink cancan outfit. It was spectacular. I paired it with some fishnet stockings and hoped for the best.

The plan worked. I made the calendar. I was thrilled. I just had to keep my eyes open for an opportunity to turn it into something bigger. That opportunity came along almost one year later. I received a call telling me the CBC wanted to use my image from the calendar in a documentary they were making. They wanted to send a producer over to my office to have me sign a waiver. This was it.

I pulled out all the pictures I had of me with other well-known people. At the time, that list was short, but it did include Ricky from the *Trailer Park Boys* and Robert Kennedy Jr. I wasn't sure who was coming from the CBC, but I planned to make it count. When she arrived—her name was Mary Munson—I went into overdrive. I told stories, gave her the elevator pitch of my life story and said I was trying to break into stand-up comedy. I signed her waiver. She left and I waited. About one week later, I got the call I had been hoping for. It was Mary Munsen and she said, "I think you would make great TV." Yes! I was sure she was about to offer me my own show. Then she told me she wanted to do a piece about me for the six o'clock news hour. I was disappointed that it wasn't something bigger, but I was smart enough to know that it was something positive. The news piece ended up being almost eight minutes long, which is pretty long for the news hour.

When it aired, a producer at CBC in Toronto saw it and contacted Mary. They came to me with the suggestion of making a documentary about my transition from law to comedy. I was off to the races. They ended up following me for about eighteen months. They even came home to northern New Brunswick with me to interview my family.

But let me catch you up on how I actually made the transition into comedy. I had never actually done stand-up. But I knew that I could make people laugh because of my time onstage at the Big Brothers Big Sisters events. So I just started letting people know that I was now a stand-up comedian. I was telling folks that if they needed an entertainer, I could fill that role. The executive director of the Nova Scotia Human Rights Commission asked me if I would do comedy for a conference she was planning for two hundred participants. I told her that I would be delighted and there would be no charge for the first gig. No charge, because I was worried I might suck and then I would feel bad taking money. I wrote a twenty-minute set, laid it down and the generous audience gave me a standing ovation. I can remember what I was wearing, what jokes I told and even the faces in the front row. I had found my thing.

Over the next six months or so, I would perform from time to time at an open mic night at Ginger's in Halifax. At the same time, I was trying to learn about the business. I have a certain way of telling a joke. In reality, I think of myself more as a humorous storyteller than a stand-up comedian. In the first year, I tried to change my style to be more like the other comics I was watching. I tried to fit myself into the predominantly white, male, under-twenty-seven group of comics who were also starting out in Halifax at the same time. I found this process very frustrating. I also wasn't getting consistent results in my performances. Russell Peters was one of the comics I was really enjoying, so I picked up a book he wrote. In it, he talked about George Carlin's advice, which was to tell the jokes that only you can tell. That was a real light-bulb moment for me.

I stopped trying to change my style. I realized there was a huge number of young, straight, white males telling jokes. But as an over-thirty, plus-size, queer Indigenous woman, I was in a much smaller group. In the same way that I have my own style, I realized I would have my own audience as well. I never did get into the club circuit or the Yuk Yuk's grind. Instead I started offering my services to the corporate world. My first actual paying gig was for a holiday party for the Confederacy of Mainland Mi'kmaq. The executive director, Don Julien, was a lovely man I had looked up to for years. The party took place at the Chow Family Restaurant in Truro, Nova Scotia . . . at noon.

I knew just about everyone in the room, so I was really nervous. I was sitting on a chair in the hallway waiting to be introduced. My nerves were on edge. I was listening to Don address his staff. He was standing under a huge Chinese lantern that was part of the restaurant's decor. "This is like a huge mistletoe.

I wonder if I will be kissed," he joked. Without hesitation, I got up off my chair, walked into the room, took Don (who is about five inches shorter than me) into my arms, laid him back and planted a big kiss on his cheek. The place erupted in laughter. In an instant, my nerves disappeared. I did my set. A few bits bombed and a few killed, but the majority of them got a decent laugh. I felt good about what I had done and even better when the cheque was placed in my hand. It was official. I was a professional comic.

Having had only positive experiences, I wondered why I heard so much about comics "dying" onstage and how hard this business is. I admit, I got pretty cocky. A few weeks later, I performed at Ginger's open mic night. There were a lot of people on the list that night. They put me later in the night, which is a compliment in the comedy world, but I don't do well sitting in the audience waiting for hours for my turn at the mic. Once I'm pumped up, I kind of have to hit the stage in the middle of my energy boost. I sat there for over three hours. I finally got to the stage at midnight. I was tired and cranky. I rushed into my first joke. The audience didn't laugh. I froze. My response was to hurry into the next joke. The audience didn't laugh. I was really getting cranky. I was pissed off at the audience, I was tired and I sped through the jokes I had planned to do and then left the stage and the bar. As Denise and I walked down the stairs to street level and out to the car, neither of us said a thing. When we finally got into the car, looking straight out the windshield down the length of Barrington Street, I said, "What a shitty crowd." Denise stayed silent. I turned to look at her and could tell she had something to say. She turned to me and said, "The audience didn't suck Candy, you did."

As you can imagine, I was furious, but from the moment I met her, Denise has always been my biggest fan, so like it or not, I knew I needed to hear what she had to say. She told me I was obviously tired and in a bad mood, and I didn't hide that from the audience. Then she told me it seemed to her that once the first two jokes bombed, I stopped trying. She, of course, was right. She woke me up to the fact that it isn't the audience's job to laugh. It's my job to make them laugh. While I've had other hard shows and tough audiences over the years, I never bombed like I did on the stage of Ginger's that night. I realized I can't sit around and wait to go on. Once I put my lipstick and lashes on, I'm ready to rock. To this day, I try to arrive as close to stage time as I can. I've learned to have a planned set, but to have a backup plan as well. Material that absolutely kills with one audience may not be at all funny to another audience, so a comic always has to be ready to change gears mid-set. It's like sex. Not every lover loves every one of your moves, you must adapt.

A few years later, I learned that a tough crowd wasn't the biggest challenge in comedy; no crowd at all was the biggest challenge. Comedy is not a solo sport. Even if you're watching your favourite comedy performance by your favourite comic, without being able to hear the audience laugh, it won't seem nearly as entertaining. What really helps a joke to land is the momentum of the laughter. There is also an incredible amount of energy and buzz that flows from an audience to the comic. So, doing comedy in an empty room is a nightmare, one I would come to be very familiar with once Covid-19 hit the world.

I was contacted by a nice lady at Waycobah First Nation in Cape Breton to perform at a conference they were hosting. She told me folks would be sitting in a conference all day, until four thirty. There would a two-hour break before dinner was served at six thirty and then a band called the Relatives would perform. They are from Eskasoni First Nation, and we have performed at a lot of events together over the years, so I know and really like these guys. But the plan was for me to come on after them. I told the organizer this would never work. First of all, once people have been in a conference all day, in their home community, you have to have dinner as soon as you break. Once people go home for two hours, the chance of them coming back for the optional activities is slim. Then in terms of the entertainment, you always put the comic before the band. Imagine an audience has been sitting in a conference all day, a two-hour break, then dinner. After dinner they get up and get dancing and burn off whatever energy they have left. And THEN, you ask them to sit down and pay attention to a comic at 11:00 p.m. It would never work.

She brought my concerns to her committee, but they insisted that the agenda stay as they had planned it. On the day of the event, I put in a full day at the office, then Denise picked me up and we started on the three-hour drive to Waycobah.

We timed it so that I would arrive just as the band was finishing their set. On the way up, in the car, I put on my stage makeup and changed my clothes: two things I have gotten very good at doing in the car over the decades I've been on the road. When we pulled into the parking lot of the community centre, I knew I was in trouble. There were four vehicles parked, two of which, I figured, had to belong to staff.

We walked into the community centre, which is a wonderful new building with lots of culture built into the design. I knew the room I would be performing in. It's a beautiful room, but it's huge, so you need to have a big crowd to fill it. Here is the scene we walked into: it was pitch black outside, so the wall of windows was in darkness, there were about twenty large, round ten-person tables in the room, and almost all of them were empty. At the very front of the room, lit up with the overflow from the stage lights, were four of the members of the Relatives. In the middle of the spotlight onstage was the lead singer sitting on a stool and the lead guitarist next to him with an acoustic guitar resting on his leg. The Relatives are a high-energy band that usually have anywhere from six to eight members. Because the room was empty, the two guys onstage were playing acoustic songs over the sound of the staff doing the dishes in the kitchen. In the back of the room, there were two old dudes who had not been at the conference but had wandered in for a meal and figured they would stay for the entertainment. Other than that, there was just the organizer, her husband and the person handling the door.

It was worse than I thought. As I made my way backstage, the Relatives were just wrapping up their last song. The rest of the band jumped up on the stage and started tearing down their gear. I asked them what they were doing. They told me they were tearing down so they could pack up and head back to Eskasoni. I wasn't scheduled to go onstage for another fifteen minutes. I said, "I don't think so, boys. Put your equipment down and go take a seat at the front-row table because there is no way I am performing to an empty room. I drove three hours to deliver this set, and damn it, I will deliver it."

For twenty minutes, I stood there and told my jokes. I told them at my regular pace and I paused for laughter. In fact, I stayed completely silent after some jokes until the ten people in the room laughed, and then I would move on to the next bit. It was a valuable skill to learn and one that I still employ. It seems counterintuitive. If no one laughs, your instinct is to move on quickly to the next joke. But I realized sometimes people need a minute to process the joke. If you move on too quickly, they don't get a chance to "get it" and laugh. Pausing for laughter can be the difference between a good set and a bad one. At the end of the night, I got my cheque, and we climbed back into the car and made the long drive home. That would be our routine for many years to come as I balanced both a day job and an entertainment career.

Early on, I was contacted by Fiona Diamond, the producer of the Halifax Comedy Festival. She wanted to see me perform. I invited her to a show I had that coming weekend.

She liked what she saw, told me some of it still needed work and invited me to be part of the Halifax Comedy Festival. I was booked on the "blue night" alongside Tim Nutt, Sugar Sammy and a handful of other comics. That was my first "big time" show. It was televised, so there was makeup and camera and stage crews. It felt like the first day of school and I was in grade one. I would be meeting some of the comics I really loved, like Steve Patterson, Mark Critch and Shaun Majumder. I hoped they would turn out to be great guys and not assholes. I was right. They were the salt of the earth. In fact, Steve Patterson dropped my name when he was being interviewed on CBC Radio about who people should come out to see. In the years since, I've had a chance to work with Steve often and I've never forgotten that he threw me a bone when I was just starting.

I arrived at the venue of the first night I was performing and apprehensively headed to makeup. I'd had other people do my makeup a couple of times before and only one person had done it in a way I liked, so I was nervous going in. I sat down in the chair of the most beautiful blonde bombshell. Her name was Anne Marie Cassidy. We began to talk and I realized she was as sweet as she was gorgeous. She had me totally relaxed and feeling confident about my set. Then she said, "There, you are ready," and she moved to the side so I could see myself in the mirror. I looked beautiful. I've worn makeup my entire adult life, but I had never made myself look this good. For me, feeling like I look my best gives me more confidence onstage. I told her, "If I ever get a TV show, I am going to find you." She smiled and we parted ways.

A few years later when *The Candy Show* got picked up, I told my production partner, "Find Anne Marie Cassidy." She was the first person we secured for the crew. She remembered what I had told her and was surprised I made good on my promise. Once I got to know Anne Marie, I realized she had been working in the film and television industry for years, so I knew I could learn from her. She taught me about light positioning and how it impacts the way a person looks on camera. One night in the first season, my mouth was incredibly dry, so dry you could hear it on the microphone. I kept taking drinks of water in between takes, but as soon as I swallowed the water, my mouth was dry again. It is common, when the cameras are being reset, for your makeup person to come in and touch up your face. They have little kits they carry over their shoulder, and usually when they are coming toward you, they either have a powder puff or a lip brush in their hands. When we cut for camera reset, Anne Marie approached me with a Styrofoam cup in her hands. When she got close enough, I saw that there were wedges of green apple inside the cup. "Eat a couple of these right now. I will explain later," she said. She was blocking the audience from seeing me. I picked up an apple wedge and bit into it. As soon as the tart Granny Smith apple hit my taste buds, my mouth filled with saliva. I smiled. She didn't have to explain. It was genius. I've shared that trick with other performers and even women going through the dry mouth of menopause. I also found out why she was so good at doing my makeup even though I was so much heavier than your average entertainer (it does make a difference in your approach). She was Rita MacNeil's makeup artist. In fact, she toured with Rita until Rita's death. My experience with Anne Marie taught me how important it is to keep your eye out for others who are operating at the top of their fields. The more of them you gather around you, the better your work will get.

Once I had that first comedy festival behind me, I felt more confident about the path I was on. Of course, people were telling me I was crazy this whole time. They told me I was crazy for walking away from law. They told me I could never start a comedy career at the age of thirty-two. They told me I was the wrong age and the wrong size for an entertainment career. But I knew they were wrong. In fact, I quickly realized the next step I wanted to take was to make the jump to television. *This Hour Has 22 Minutes* was shot live in Halifax. I thought it would be awesome if I could get a gig writing for that show or doing a guest spot. At that time, a dear friend of mine had a son who had graduated from Saint Mary's University and started filming a fake reality show with his two buddies. The guy was Robb Wells, better known as Ricky, and of course the show was the *Trailer Park Boys*. I thought it would be cool to get a little guest spot on that show. I mean, I had always dreamed of having my own show. I had the concept all worked out and even had a name for it. I would call it *The Candy Show*. But I figured I would have to start small and work my way up to that point. As it turned out, the closest I got to *22 Minutes* was meeting Cathy Jones at the Halifax Comedy Festival, and I couldn't make any headway with the *Trailer Park Boys,* either (spoiler alert: later, I had a recurring role in season 10), but I DID get *The Candy Show.* I was doing what I loved and what made me happy.

SCENE 15

The one where I birth
The Candy Show

As I was building my entertainment career, I was still spending forty hours per week at a day job. I stayed with Aboriginal Affairs for a few years. The part of the work I really enjoyed was travelling to every First Nation in Nova Scotia. I made great friends in every community and really got to know the Mi'kmaq of Nova Scotia, my adopted province. But I was finding some elements of the work very frustrating. I wanted to work in a larger department where there would be more diversity among the staff. Sadly, Aboriginal Affairs only had two Aboriginal people working there and neither of us were in senior positions. I went from there to the Public Service Commission in the position of provincial diversity officer. This was a bigger department, but it was even more homogeneous than Aboriginal Affairs had been. There is a new word being used right now to describe a certain kind of person: "Karen." Well, at that department, I had to deal with a whole lot of Karens. I knew I wouldn't last there long because no matter how good you are at anti-racism work, you can't wake people who are convinced they are already woke. I finally landed at the Department of Education, where I was working directly on Mi'kmaq education. I thought this was a position I could use to make a difference for my community. I could be an advocate from the inside. Early on in that endeavour, Albert Marshall, one of the Elders I most cherished, told me the work would burn me out. I insisted that I could do it. He said, "Candy, no man can serve two masters." Gender specificity aside, he was right. But I did get some important work done at the department, work that I am really proud of. This is just to remind you that while I was trying to make all these entertainment moves, I was also managing a highly stressful career as a public servant. And I was making some pretty important decisions in my private life around this time, too.

Denise had been at the same veterinary clinic for thirteen years. She really liked her boss, the veterinarian who owned the clinic, but she was getting frustrated with not being able to advance. I suggested that a change might be as good as a rest.

So she took a position at a clinic closer to our new home in Cole Harbour, where she became even more frustrated and she didn't agree with the kind of medicine being practised. She was getting more and more vocal about her frustration while she was at work, and at home, she was talking about how unhappy she was professionally.

One night in bed, I asked her what she really wanted to do. She told me she always wanted to be a real estate agent. I suggested she go for it, but she was too scared to quit her job. Her parents divorced when she was very young, which had forced Denise to grow up fast. Denise's father died when she was twenty, and her mother was someone who depended on her, not someone she could depend upon. So, she had always been independent. And even though I was working both a day job and gigging, she just couldn't bring herself to quit her job. The real estate course was costly and it would take almost two months to complete, during which time she would not be working. At that point, we still had separate bank accounts and we each paid half of all the bills.

Sometimes when you are hesitating to make a necessary jump, the universe comes along and gives you a push. She got fired on Thanksgiving weekend. She had been pushing back at work a lot. She'd gone to school for three years to get her certification and she was a top-notch technician who had worked for years with a top-notch veterinarian who recognized her skills, but at this clinic she was being asked to make the coffee. She felt the shifts were not being doled out fairly. She often was scheduled to work on holidays and weekends. I was planning to get a ride home for Thanksgiving, with my friend Wyatt, whose family lives just a few minutes up the road from mine. We were hoping Denise could come with us, but when the schedule came out on Thursday, once again she found out she was working the long weekend. She left a note at work for her boss Thursday night, indicating how unfair she thought the scheduling was. She was scheduled to work at noon on Friday. Wyatt had picked me up early that morning and we started out for northern New Brunswick. We were about an hour into our drive when Denise called me on my cell phone to tell me she was fired. I told her not to worry about it, that I would take care of it, and I instructed her to pack her bag for the weekend. We turned the car around and drove back into Cole Harbour to get her. This was one of the many times since leaving law that my experience as a lawyer has come in handy. As we were driving back to get her, I called her boss. I was very cordial and informed him that he just fired her without cause, which was illegal, so he would have to pay. He could either sit down and negotiate a settlement with me or we could go to court. It wouldn't cost me anything either way as I wouldn't need to hire a lawyer. Even though he was in the wrong, I advised him not to take my word for it and to call an employment lawyer to get some advice over the weekend. I gave him until Tuesday.

He got the advice. His lawyer told him exactly the same thing I had said, and we worked out a settlement. He ended up paying for the cost of Denise's real estate course and he gave her the money she needed to survive while taking the course. I always say that when something "bad" happens, be ready for the gift it is actually bringing your way. Denise might never have had the nerve to quit and would have stayed in a job where she was miserable. But because she was fired, she entered an exciting new career, one she was very gifted in, and her income quadrupled in her first year (which led to us buying our dream home).

By then I was in my late thirties, so another major personal decision had to be made sooner rather than later. Would I, or would I not, have kids? All my life I dreamed of being a mother. I dressed all my dolls every day as a child and tucked them into bed every night. By the time I was a teen, I told my parents I was going to have lots of kids but I didn't want a husband (which used to drive my father around the bend). In my twenties, I knew it wasn't the right time for children. I wasn't financially stable enough and I wasn't sure George was the right partner to have kids with. He had told me so many stories about what he was like as a boy, and I worried that if I had a son, he might take the same path. When I first met Denise, she told me she would never give birth to a baby but she would be open to having kids if I wanted to carry them.

As you know, parenting was my mother's full-time professional gig. When you have a blueprint like that, it is hard to imagine yourself making the grade. I thought about it and thought about it. There was no way I could continue to pursue my entertainment career with all the time spent on the road and parent the way I would want to. My mom had said to me more than once, "Yes, I had you at forty-three, but trust me, that is a young woman's game." I had already gained a considerable amount of weight, enough that it would have been a health risk for me to get pregnant without making some major changes. It was difficult. I lost a lot of sleep and shed a lot of tears. But I made the decision not to have children. At different times, I've thought that I made a mistake, but on the whole, looking at my life's arc, I know I made the right decision given the way my life has progressed. But sacrifices have to be made when you are running down a dream.

A big part of that dream was *The Candy Show*. Growing up in Point La Nim, we only had two English television channels until I was well into junior high, and basically, for radio, CKNB out of Campbellton was it. On a clear night, I could sometimes get a radio station from Presque Isle, Maine, on my transistor radio. But that was it, so when it came to music, I relied on magazines like *Rolling Stone* and *Hit Parader*. I would wait with bated breath every week for *The New Music* to come on TV hosted by Jeanne Beker (a personal idol of mine) and later, the mullet-haired J.D. Roberts, who turned into John Roberts, a serious newsman on US television. When I did see interviews with bands I liked on talk shows or *American Bandstand*, I was never satisfied with the questions they were asked. I felt like either the interviewer didn't know anything about the band in question or didn't know how to listen. There is nothing worse than when the interviewee says something profound or incredibly interesting and the interviewer just rolls on to the next question on their sheet. I used to think, while sitting in my little pink bedroom, wouldn't it be cool if the bands could play right here in my bedroom and then they could just hang out with me on my bed and we could have real conversations.

One of my friends in high school, Derek Maher, had a very cool bedroom; it took up the entire lower floor of his house. His bed was angled in the centre of the room, and on it was a fitted sheet and a black faux bear skin. My pink room was spectacular, but I only had a single bed, so when I imagined those performances and interviews, I would imagine them taking place in my room, but with Derek's bed setup.

Like just about every comedian of the past seventy years, I loved *The Tonight Show.* I thought Johnny Carson had the best job in television, followed closely by Oprah. There had never been a nightly Canadian live show until Mike Bullard came along. When I was in law school, that show was a treat for when I was studying all night. I would take a one-hour break before bedtime to watch *Open Mike with Mike Bullard.* I loved the episode when he had my favourite vocalist of all time, Burton Cummings, on. Bullard was, in my opinion, living the dream. The show I was imagining for myself would look very different from his, but he showed me that such a show was possible in Canada.

In the same way that I just started telling people I was a comedian, I started saying to everyone I met from the entertainment industry, "Let me tell you about *The Candy Show.*"

Seriously, even if I found out you were the lady that delivered sandwiches on set, I would tell you about *The Candy Show*. I received a call from a producer at CBC TV who wanted me to come in and audition for a show she was working on. While at the audition, I, of course, told her about *The Candy Show*. I thought the audition went well, but later that night, she called me to tell me they went another way. While she was on the phone, though, she told me that she was starting a production company of her own and wanted to know more about *The Candy Show*. I told her my concept and we set up a meeting to discuss it in more detail.

She was starting the company with a partner and they were interested in the show. We had a lot of differences creatively on how we saw the show, but we agreed on enough of it to get money from the Aboriginal Peoples Television Network (APTN) to shoot a pilot. I was beside myself with joy. I didn't know anything about making television, so I had to rely on my partner for that side of it. I started planning what guests I wanted and the feel I wanted the show to have. I was bound and determined to have a live house band. We got a handful of players from Halifax—all really great guys—and we picked a venue, which was The Marquee Club in Halifax. We decided to sell tickets and I was so thankful that Addition Elle provided my wardrobe.

My mother came down to see the pilot. In fact, on the morning of the pilot, the phone woke us up. It was bad news. Her only sister had died. I thought she might want to go home,

but she said, "No, I won't miss your pilot." My biggest concern was that no one would show up and there would be no
live audience. Thankfully, people were lined up around the
building. We weren't sure everyone was going to be able to fit
inside the venue! While there were lots of people I knew, there
were lots I didn't know. The deputy minister of the Department
of Education, Dennis Cochrane, came along with the senior
management team from my day job. I couldn't see the whole
crowd that night, but I was thrilled to find out that Cathy Jones
from *22 Minutes* was there along with her main squeeze at the
time, Tom Wilson from Blackie and the Rodeo Kings.

Downtown Halifax crowds at that time were pretty white.
I was thrilled to see how diverse the audience was that night.
Long-time Canadian journalist Silver Donald Cameron was
there and wrote about the show in the Halifax *Chronicle Her-
ald*. The first thing he commented on was the packed audience. He described it as such: "They were young and old; gay
and straight, Black, White, Indigenous and Asian, all brought
together by a common taste and attitude." He couldn't have
paid me a greater compliment. This was my baby. This was my
brainchild and it was happening.

There were a whole bunch of technical glitches, like my
microphone not working when I walked out onstage to start
the show. But overall, I thoroughly enjoyed the night. It did,
indeed, feel like a dream come true. My hope was that the
magic was caught on tape. Alas, it wasn't. The final product
was disappointing. I wasn't properly lit; in fact, at one point

in the show, it looks like my face and hands are floating in mid-air. It didn't have the look or the feel that I had expected. The network gave us $85,000 for the pilot, from which I drew a salary of twelve hundred bucks, so I expected to see the rest of that budget reflected onscreen. I was so worried I might have screwed up my chance with this pilot. We submitted what we had and waited.

And boy, did we wait. I wanted to have a party on the night it aired to celebrate my television debut. We only found out a day in advance about the airing, and it ended up just being Denise and me alone at our house watching. On top of there being no fanfare, we were so disappointed with how it looked. At that point, I really thought I screwed up my chance. After it aired, we didn't hear anything from the network. Six months went by; then twelve months later, we still hadn't heard. At that point, I resigned myself to the fact that this attempt at show biz was a failure. About eighteen months after the pilot aired, Denise and I were in Seattle to see Pink on her first American tour when the call came in. APTN wanted six episodes for the first season of *The Candy Show*. I was thirty-nine years old.

The one where the universe keeps me humble

When we were living in the Rawdon hills, I started to notice an occasional kink in my right groin area. It would come for a few days and then disappear for a couple of months, so I really didn't pay much attention to it. When we bought our first house together on Westfield Crescent in Cole Harbour, the kink started occurring more frequently and it would stay for longer periods of time. Having spent so much of my young life doing the splits off first base on the softball field, and having the occasional bad fall on the ski hill that would pull my groin, I assumed this was just a little hitch in my giddy-up associated with my athletic childhood. As time went on, the kink was becoming increasingly painful. One of the things I inherited from my dad is a high pain threshold, so even though it was increasing, I could handle the pain. So it didn't dawn on me that it might be something I needed to see a doctor about.

After Denise's first, very successful year as a real estate agent, we made another move. She was showing a client the specs of a condo in a new development in downtown Halifax. The development, in the North End of the city, consisted of two towers and a string of ten houses along Gladstone Street. One day, we were in the area and she brought me into the show home to see it. I fell in love. From the moment I walked in the front door of this 3,000-square-foot retro-style house, I knew it had to be ours. The front door opened up into a long entrance hall that gave me the first glimpse of the thirteen-foot ceilings. There was a formal living room in the front of the main floor, a TV lounge, dining room and powder room. The kitchen opened out onto the back deck, fenced yard and driveway. On the second floor of the house, at the top of the beautiful oak staircase, was a huge master bedroom with an ensuite that contained a bathtub so long that Denise never could bathe in it because she kept floating around. As a life-long bath enthusiast, I must say that it was the best tub I ever had. There was a smaller bedroom, a large bedroom at the front of the house and another full bathroom. The finished basement, which had loads of windows and its own entrance, was a huge open space in which we placed another bedroom, an office and a second kitchen.

We crunched the numbers and put our Westfield house on the market. If we could sell our place, we would put in an offer on the dream home. After two weeks of nail biting, someone made an offer, and one month later, we moved into the home of my dreams. About one hundred people attended our house-warming party, and still the place wasn't crowded. One of the great advantages of the house was that it was within walking distance of my office at the Department of Education. The first Monday in the new house, I pulled on a pair of sneakers, threw my work shoes in my bag and started out on my one kilometre walk to work.

As soon as I hit the sidewalk, I could feel my kink start to act up. By the time I got halfway across the Halifax Common, the kink had turned into searing pain. And by the time I got to the office, I had a limp. Once I sat down at my desk, I thought the pain would go away; instead it worsened. I called Denise to pick me up after work and made an appointment to see my doctor. I still assumed it was an old injury flare-up and that a couple of sessions with a physiotherapist would have me right as rain again. My doctor sent me for some X-rays of my hips, after which I headed to Cape Breton for some meetings. I was in the lobby of the Cambridge Suites in Cape Breton when my doctor called me and told me I had advanced osteoarthritis and she was pretty sure my right hip had to be replaced, but she wanted to send me to a specialist to confirm. I wasn't forty yet and couldn't quite process what I was hearing. I couldn't think of anything less rock and roll than an artificial hip. And I didn't know they even did such operations on people as young as I was.

She sent me to see Dr. Reg Yabsley, who incidentally was the first doctor in Canada to perform a hip replacement. He had been jabbed by a needle in the operating room years earlier and contracted Hepatitis C. As a result, he was no longer performing surgeries but was an arthritis consultant. Denise and I were sitting in the waiting room when I saw this mad scientist–looking man in a doctor's coat come out of the exam room. He was gruff and I mistakenly thought he was going to be grumpy. I had an uneasy feeling, while Denise liked him instantly. As soon as we got into the exam room, he turned to me and said, "Imagine this, the famous columnist Candy Palmater in my exam room." He was lovely. Intelligent, playful, warm and a bit quirky is how I would describe him, which are some of my favourite qualities in a human being. A few years ago, he took a tour of cuckoo clocks in Germany, and in his spare time he carves wooden bears. Not your average surgeon. Despite all of my protestations, he agreed with my family doctor, my right hip had to be replaced. He showed me the X-rays, and even to my untrained eye, I could see that there was no cartilage left in my hip joint. I could see that the top of my femur was sort of mashed into the bone of my hip.

Dr. Yabsley did two great things for me that day. First, he told me to get over myself and buy a cane. "You walking around with this pronounced limp makes you look far older than a cane will," he told me. He was right. I bought myself a leopard-print cane and started getting used to my new reality. The second great thing he did was refer me to Dr. Michael Dunbar.

I had asked Dr. Yabsley if the arthritis was caused by my years as an athlete or by being overweight for the past eight years. He told me that although both may have sped up the onset, neither was to blame. "Go home and thank your parents for the great teeth and the shitty joints. Arthritis was in the cards for you, no matter what your lifestyle would have been." He did inform me, however, that the heavier I was, the more intense the pain would be. He assured me that the success of replacement surgery relies greatly on the skill of the surgeon. He told me he knew Michael Dunbar as a young boy and mentored him in his career. Not only did he refer me to Dr. Dunbar, he put a call in to the good doctor to personally pass my file on to him.

When I met with Dr. Dunbar, he told me I would decide when the hip would be replaced and that I would make the decision when I could no longer stand the pain. Mechanically, the hip was done and he was ready to replace it, but he understood my hesitancy. I was the wild child. The cool aunt. The sex-driven flirt. Now I was going to be the old lady with the artificial hip? Not sexy. He told me to let him know when I was ready. The pain progressed, and doing simple things like putting the sock on my right foot or driving for more than ten minutes became impossible. I began to rely on Denise for a lot of my day-to-day needs. Eventually, I realized that asking your wife for assistance putting your sock on isn't exactly sexy either!

That trip to Seattle was a tipping point. Although the Pink concert was general admission and we got there early enough that we could have stood right near the stage (my favourite place to watch concerts), we had to sit in the lower bowl—my hip wouldn't hold me through a full concert. In fact, a few weeks later, back in Halifax, we went to an outdoor Kiss concert (dressed in full Kiss makeup and costume), and halfway through the show, I had to lower myself to the ground near a back fence to watch it.

So, when the call came that *The Candy Show* was getting picked up for a first season, I had two urgent problems that needed solving. I had to get this hip replaced before we went to production and I needed to find a production partner who was experienced in managing a full, independent television production. I knew all the things I wanted improved from the pilot, but I didn't know how to make them happen. I needed to find a partner who had the skill and experience to help me achieve my goal and one that was comfortable with me having creative control of the show. I researched a number of production companies in Halifax and decided to approach Ocean Entertainment. They had great success with Chef Michael Smith's television shows and a handful of other productions. They had won a couple of Geminis along the way.

This is when I started to really learn about the business side of entertainment. While I will always be thankful to my first production partners for helping me get the go-ahead for the pilot and for believing in me as a pretty unknown entity, I knew I needed to find a production company that could bring my concept to the next level. This was my chance and I wanted to succeed or fail with a product that was creatively all mine. It was difficult to make the break. Although they were paid handsomely, I think they were hurt by me moving on. But those are the hard decisions we all have to make in order to chase after our dreams.

I went in and met with the president of Ocean Entertainment, Johanna Elliot. In the world of TV, it was a gift of sorts. I walked in with the budget in hand and the go-ahead for the first season, so there was everything to gain and nothing to lose for Ocean. I liked Johanna's vibe from the get-go. She was about my age, tall, slender and all business. Once I got to know her, she also revealed a wonderfully warm side. I liked the combination. She had a business manager with a great head for numbers and a production manager who knew how to put a crew together.

What we needed to really bring my vision to life was a strong director. We tossed a couple of names around, including Mike Clattenburg of *Trailer Park Boys* fame. Although all of us in the room were throwing around names we knew from other series, Johanna kept bringing up Trevor Grant. He was from Saskatchewan and had worked on a number of her other shows. I agreed to meet him. My main concern was I wanted someone who was going to respect my vision and not try to turn the show into something that wasn't me. Trevor flew in from Saskatchewan and came over to our house so we could meet and spend some time together. We both wanted to see if we were compatible. We had a martini together, and as we spoke, I think we both realized we were going to work great together. I didn't know it at the time, but I had just found the next Emery Johnson in my life.

We knew we had about six months before we had to shoot. All I needed was a hip. I told Dr. Dunbar that I would be ready at the drop of a hat. I would take a cancelled appointment, a last-minute spot, anything. A couple of days before Christmas, his secretary called and said he could put my new hip in on his last day before the Christmas break. It just happened that it fell on Denise's birthday, December 18. Because my weight makes it risky, I never like to be put under anesthesia, so I requested to be awake for the procedure. Also, the lawyer in me wanted to know if someone said oops during my surgery!

I wasn't worried about anything peripheral as I was going into the surgery. My day job had a great benefits package. I would be paid my full salary for the six weeks I would be off work. My benefits also covered the rental of a hospital bed in my house, the raised toilets seats and other accommodations. I was fully covered, so my only worry was the surgery and its outcome. Denise and I arrived at the hospital at about 9:00 a.m. They finally took me into the operating room around one in the afternoon. Dr. Dunbar's music was already playing. It was a great mix of eighties hits. "Your Love" by The Outfield was on as he started sawing off the top of my femur. I had an epidural on board but was fully conscious, so I proceeded to basically run two hours of material to keep everyone laughing as the surgery went on. At one point, the intern who was holding my leg at a strange angle said, "If she doesn't stop, I'm going to drop her leg!" Once the new hip was in, Dr. Dunbar told me it was "nothing but net." In other words, it went perfectly. I was thrilled with the level of care I received in the OR and was happy the procedure went well. Little did I know, it was going to get a whole lot worse before it got better. The epidural wore off while I was still in the operating room. In fact, I could feel about the last ten staples of the forty-five he had put in me. The nurses in recovery would not accept that I was feeling pain. They said epidurals don't wear off that quickly. As the intense pain of surgery set deeper and deeper into my hip and leg, I continued to plead with them for painkillers. Finally, one of them held up a blanket so I could not see my legs. The other took an ice chip out of a Styrofoam cup and touched me with it. She asked if I could say where she had touched me. I told her it was the inside of my left ankle. She shared a nervous glance with her colleague, then touched me again and looked at me. I told her the ice was now touching my right knee. They both looked at me and said, "The epidural has worn off." Well, no kidding, that is what I had been saying for over an hour. Unfortunately, pain works in mysterious ways. If you get painkillers on board before the pain gets bad, you can control it quite easily, but once it sets in, it is very hard to get a hold on it.

The next three days were pure hell. At about 7:00 p.m. on the third evening, a sweet nurse came in to give me my morphine shot. As soon as she left, I could feel incredible relief. My whole body seemed to unclench for the first time since surgery. When Denise came in to see me, she was surprised at just how serene my face looked. She had no sooner remarked about it when the nurse came back in, in a panic. She had given me three times the amount of morphine I was supposed to get. I told her not to do anything about it because I was finally free of pain. She told Denise to watch me and to make sure that I was taking at least a couple of breaths a minute . . . seriously, that stuff makes you so chilled out, you forget to breathe. There would be one power puke over a nurse and some very inconvenient diarrhea before I finally got out of the hospital, but I was moving in the right direction. And thank goodness for it, because I had a show to shoot, and that was right around the corner.

The one where my parents are proud of me

The first two weeks after my replacement, I was sure I had made a mistake in going through with the operation. I stood on the hip twenty-four hours after surgery and walked up a flight of stairs forty-eight hours after the operation. Three days later I went home. I was in excruciating pain and I was feeling increasingly depressed. I couldn't understand my emotional state because I am someone who is always optimistic. The next day, my doctor told me to stop taking the pain meds I was on because they were causing the depression. I switched to Tylenol, and sure enough, within twenty-four hours I was myself again. Two weeks later the pain was receding and I realized this surgery was the best decision I could have made.

As I was healing, we started having pre-production meetings for *The Candy Show*. Our first hurdle was figuring out where we would shoot the show. We settled on a spot that had a special history for me. The Lebanese church in Halifax owns a large centre that houses a bingo hall called Olympic Bingo. That name is a throwback to its original name. Back in 1967, when my oldest brother Billy used to go to this spot, it was a bar called The Olympic (colloquially known as The Dirty O) and that is where, before I was born, he met his wife Aloyse.

The first two years of *The Candy Show* were shot while I still had my day job. I would book my two-week vacation, and we would get the entire season shot over a seven-day period. It was a hectic pace but I was so excited that my dream was being realized. My only sadness, as we started to shoot the first season, was the fact that my family couldn't be there to see it. Early during the first day on set, we were shooting what we called "Pieces of Candy." These were small clips in which I spoke about the artists coming on the show or other intimate thoughts. My director asked me what it would mean to me if my family could be there to see it. I tried to answer but got choked up. He told me to look over my shoulder. There was my mom and my two sisters. Then I really started to cry. I was so touched that my sister Sharron planned this whole surprise trip. She told Denise they were coming but they all kept it hidden from me. I was so touched to have them there, to be part of this wonderful moment in my life.

What would have made this moment entirely complete is if my dad could have been there, too. He may have had a lot of opinions about women while I was growing up, and my feminist ways made a lot of waves. My mother told me again and again, "You'll never change him, just let it go." But I could never let any of it go and I kept insisting that my father was too smart to be that dumb. For years, we butted heads. But when CBC was filming that documentary about my life, they came home to the North Shore with me, and one of the interviews they did was with Daddy. By then, he was in the old people's home with dementia and Alzheimer's. I told them they would likely not get much out of him, but they said they wanted to try. Mommy and I went to the home with them, and they set up in Daddy's room. No matter what the producer was asking him, he was talking about the war and a myriad of other things. Finally, I think the producer realized they weren't going to get much more out of him, and she said, "One more question, Mr. Palmater. What do you think is the best thing about Candy?" Daddy's eyes seemed to focus and he said, "I guess the fact that she is female." My mother and I looked at one another in surprise. We were both wondering where this was going when Daddy said, "Women don't get credit for things, but Candy always made sure she got credit. So, on some level, that must be good for all women." He paused for a moment and then he said, "Kids are always idle. They play a lot. Not my baby. She was always planning her next move. I won't live to see them all but I know she isn't done yet." And just like, that he flipped back into talking about the war.

By the time my mom and I got the car, I was crying. She always told me I couldn't change him, but at eighty-six, he had a feminist thought. He died a few months later. It was such a gift to know that in spite of all the haggling, somewhere deep down inside him, he understood who I was and why. That was such a gift.

So I know, even though he wasn't with us that day with my mom and my sisters, he was proud of me.

Although everything wasn't perfect in that first season, I was still over the moon that I had my own show. We shot six episodes in the first season. The set wasn't quite what I wanted yet and the live audience was small, but we had some great artists on the show and I learned so much. Up to that point in my career, I never "rehearsed" my comedy. I would sit at happy hour with friends and hold court. During those Friday nights, I often worked out my material, but I always felt it was better if I didn't rehearse, but just let it flow. Trevor insisted that I rehearse the monologues, even if it was just the two of us at the rehearsals. I pushed back at him but he insisted. What a difference it made.

If you watch Season 1 of *The Candy Show* and then watch Season 5, you will see a huge level of improvement, both in my skills and also the look of the show. Trevor is responsible for that improvement. Trevor could see my talent, he understood and believed in my vision and he had the skill to bring me to the next level. He was my creative partner in all aspects of the show.

Every episode of the show started with a monologue from me, then featured a performing artist and a musical guest. I loved to try things with my guests. Over the course of the show, I had my hands set on fire, I did a lift with an acrobat, I belly danced and I also played drums, bass guitar, guitar, saxophone and cello.

By Season 3, the set was really starting to come together. It was a wonderland of pink. We built my dressing room right next to the audience so there was only a curtain separating me from the crowd. This allowed me to hear and feel the energy of the audience as I was getting ready to start the show. The audience was filled to capacity for each and every show. People came out dressed in their best and ready for a good time. We created an oasis of acceptance and joy inside our studio. I loved looking out to see an older conservative couple nestled around a table with two guys covered in face tattoos, everyone talking to one another and feeling at ease. We shot two episodes every night with an intermission in between when folks would head upstairs to where we had a bar and I would arrange for what I call "church lady" sandwiches.

Each day, I arrived on set at about 11:00 a.m. In the first few seasons, Denise would drive me to the set; after that, we had a driver pick me up and bring me to the set. I liked being there early in the day to be with the crew as they were getting ready for the night and to meet with Trevor for a final creative session. Denise arrived mid-afternoon to set up her station, where she sold merchandise and worked the door. You had to have tickets to get in, but the tickets were free. Denise also took care of ticket distribution ahead of production. The only "price" to get in was a food item for the foodbank. I am proud to say over the five seasons of *The Candy Show*, we brought in thousands of pounds of food for the hungry in our city.

The guests on the show would arrive midday and would run through a full dress rehearsal so Trevor could get close-up shots of their performances. I loved watching these performances and it gave me an idea of what the performance would look like during the live show. In Season 5, we had a classical quartet on the show. We had a plan for me to get a cello lesson from the cellist, Shimon Walt. My producers told me I would need to rent a cello because his cello was a $250,000 instrument with a $30,000 bow, and there was little chance that he would allow me to even hold it, never mind play it. So we rented a cheap cello and I was all ready for my classical lesson. During the dress rehearsal, I sat on my bed on the stage, which was about three feet away from where the quartet was playing. They came onstage and took their seats. Now all my life I have been around musicians. I've dated them, sat around at band practice and hung out backstage. Never have I had close contact with classical music. Yes, I go to the symphony often and I see live ballet regularly, but I am sitting in the audience separated by the formality of the performance. And there I was, sitting a couple of feet away when they began to play an Argentinian tango. I was unexpectedly overcome with emotion. I began to weep uncontrollably. It was so embarrassing. When the tears first started to fall, my sound engineer, Neil, was standing near the bed and we made eye contact with one another. He told me later he knew exactly what was happening. When the song was done, I jumped off the bed, ducked backstage, got myself together and came back out to apologize. I told the members of the quartet not to worry, that I would keep myself together for the live show. The music was just so beautiful.

That night during the live show, they played their piece and then I called for my rental cello so I could get my lesson. Shimon said, "No, anyone who was moved by our music the way you were this afternoon must know what a real cello feels like." He sat me on his chair at centre stage. I was wearing a charcoal dress with a full skirt and bright red John Fleuvog shoes. I planted my feet wide apart. He smiled as he handed his cello to me and said, "She is my lover, be very gentle with her. Now press her to your chest and pull the bow across the strings." I hugged that beautifully crafted instrument whose wood was so smooth and shiny against the full length of my torso and gently pulled the bow across the strings. What was remarkable was not the sound but the feeling. I could feel those notes vibrating over my ribs and my belly, and it felt like I was one with the instrument, as though we were making that sound together, our big, rounded bodies vibrating in unison. It was a feeling I still think about when I close my eyes. Shimon then put his arms around me from behind, his hands on my hands, and we proceeded to play "Twinkle, Twinkle, Little Star" on a $250,000 cello. What a moment.

Back to how a day looked when we shot the show. After the dress rehearsal, I would sit in my makeup chair, and the process of doing my hair and makeup would start as I reviewed my notes. I never like to go onstage after having a full meal because I am always scared of being halfway through a show and needing to use the bathroom, but I do need energy for the long evening onstage, so at about 4:00 p.m., the crew would break and a hot meal was provided for them by our catering. They gathered upstairs to eat together. At that time, our craft person, Jenny Reeves, would bring me one perfect egg salad sandwich on white bread, plated with little bits of raw vegetables cut to look like flowers. This moment felt like home for me because I could taste the love Jenny put into my preshow snack. After the meal, the crew would get ready for showtime. By then, the audience would be lined up outside the building waiting to get in. The air was electric. I would start dressing in my room just off the stage. Just before the doors opened, our *Candy Show* soundtrack would start blasting through the venue. This soundtrack was a compilation of songs with the word candy in them. It was high energy, and to this day when I hear those songs, my adrenaline starts to spike.

As the audience filed in, my excitement grew with theirs. Their energy was infectious. The show sequence was set in motion. Trevor would come in to have a last-minute talk, while my hair and makeup was being given the final touches, and Dan, one of my sound engineers, would wire me up (i.e., hide the microphone pack inside my clothes). Then the magic moment would happen. Everyone would leave the dressing room. I was all alone behind the curtain. The crowd would start to chant my name. I would stand right behind the curtain so the glow of the roving spotlight would bleed through and wash over my face, then my theme song would start to play. In that moment, my energy would soar, and in my mind, I would really try to feel that moment and know that when the curtains opened, everything I had dreamed of would be happening.

For the final season of the show, I brought my entire family to Halifax and put them up at a hotel so they could all experience the show with me. By then, my mother was in her late eighties and sitting through two episodes was hard for her. After the first episode, she asked my sister if she would take her back to the hotel, which would mean my sister would miss the second episode. In my dressing room, I had a very long and comfortable couch, so I offered it to Mommy. She could stretch out there, sleep if she needed to, but she would still be able to hear the show. She agreed. I got her snuggled into my couch with a pink duvet covering her. She was lying so she could see me at my vanity and at the curtain before the second show. There was a soft light right above her face that made her eyes twinkle. Once I was sure she was comfortable, I carried on with my routine. The room filled with people doing all the last-minute preshow things. During that time, I forgot she was there. Then the room emptied out, the lights went down, the music surged and the crowd started to chant my name. As the spotlights started to wash over my face, I remembered Mommy was there. I turned my head toward her quickly, and in that moment, our eyes locked. She had tears in her eyes and a true look of wonder on her face.

It was a split second, but so much passed between us. After a lifetime of sacrifice and selflessness to the benefit of her children, in that moment, she got to ride the wave of my life. She got to experience the pure unadulterated joy my life had become. She gave me the most beautiful smile, and then I turned back toward the sound, the curtains opened and out I went.

It was one of the most beautiful experiences of my life. They say when you are about to die, your life flashes before you. For me that moment will be in my final montage. When those days come that I miss her so badly I feel like my heart will break, I close my eyes and relive that moment in my mind.

I'm older now and she has passed, but for that one moment in time, Mommy saw the dream from my eyes, and in that moment, she knew her baby was fully formed and well on her way to running down her dream.

Afterword

I t's an odd feeling to read Candy's final words. Her incredible storytelling brings her alive in so many ways. If only this could be physically true. Candy had five glorious seasons of *The Candy Show* on APTN. Immediately afterward, she graced the set of *Trailer Park Boys*, then went on to host CBC Radio One's *q*, which led to her own show on CBC Radio, *The Candy Palmater Show*. And she kept chasing her dreams with countless comedy shows, festivals and speaking tours, including an "in conversation" partnership with Seneca College. Candy was a powerful, unique and thought-provoking speaker, connecting with people of all ages and backgrounds, often moving them to tears.

Despite the lockdowns over the pandemic, Candy continued to connect with her fans as a recurring guest cohost on CTV's *The Social* and as a panelist on *Because News* and *The Next Chapter* on CBC Radio. She loved these shows tremendously and she was well-loved back. It did not end there. In 2021, Candy hit the set of a new CBC sitcom *Run the Burbs*. We had more new projects in the hopper for Candy. Her dream to sing . . . well, folks, I wish you could have seen the sizzle reel for this show about an aging punk rock star! She was made to sing punk rock.

Candy adored her multi-faceted life in all ways. The point she made living each day was to never stop running down your dream. Even when you achieve greatness, keep going. Enjoy the ride along the way, too. Candy certainly did. And if you keep failing miserably, at least you're trying. If you take anything away from this book, it should be Candy's philosophy: It's never too late, you will fail and you are enough as you are right now in this moment. So, what are you waiting for. . . . Run down your own dream!

—Denise Tompkins
April 2022

MISSING-PERSON INFORMATION

If anyone has information on the whereabouts of Darryl Ferneyhough, last seen at NRG night club on Gottingen Street, Halifax, Nova Scotia, on May 13, 2001, please contact your local police service or Crime Stoppers.

Halifax Rainbow Encyclopedia: Darryl Ferneyhough (hfxns.org).